BLACK PRIDE AND BLACK PREJUDICE

BLACK PRIDE AND BLACK PREJUDICE

Paul M. Sniderman

and

Thomas Piazza

PRINCETON UNIVERSITY PRESS   Princeton and Oxford

#49226203

Library of Congress Cataloging-in Publication Data

Sniderman, Paul M.
Black pride and black prejudice / Paul M. Sniderman and Thomas
Piazza.
p.   cm.
Includes bibliographical references and index.
ISBN 0-691-09261-3 (acid-free paper)
1. African Americans—Race identity.   2. African Americans—
Attitudes. 3. Prejudices—United States.   4. United States—Race
relations.   I. Piazza, Thomas Leonard.   II. Title.
E185.625 .S65 2002
305.896'073—dc21   2002023661

British Library Cataloging-in-Publication Data is available

This book has been composed in Stone

Printed on acid-free paper. ∞
www.pupress.princeton.edu

Printed in the United States of America

10   9   8   7   6   5   4   3   2   1

TO KAREN GARRETT 1950–1999

Contents

List of Figures

List of Tables

P refaces are a way for a writer to speak informally to a potential reader, to say, Here is what I actually set out to do,
what I really am trying to say. That is a bit of a problem for us. The
issues we deal with invite misunderstanding. A sample: Does taking
pride in being black lead black Americans to qualify their identity as
Americans? Is there a problem of black anti-Semitism? If there is, is
it tied in any significant measure to taking pride in being black?
Does valuing being black encourage blacks to devalue those who are
not black? If our answers to these questions are not clear and com-
pelling, nothing we say here will excuse what we say later.

And there is another potential problem. Instead of just conduct-
ing a standard public opinion interview, our study carries out a
number of custom-designed, randomized experiments. That is the
strength of the study. Randomized experiments have an inferential
power that no other procedure has, and many of our experiments—
the SAT experiment is a flagship example—are original, allowing us
to see some things that it has not been possible to see before. Yet
there is good reason to be cautious about things being done for the
first time.

We therefore have worked hard to test our findings. As a rule we
designed and carried out experiments in pairs. For example, one
question we investigated is whether black Americans are as willing
to support policies like affirmative action when nonblacks are their
beneficiaries as when blacks are. So we carried out a pair of experiments, one focusing on affirmative action for jobs, the other for congressional representation, each contrasting support for the policies
when blacks benefit or when Mexican Americans do. Just so far as
the results of the two experiments are similar—and as it happens

they are nearly identical—one can have confidence that the findings are reliable.

It was not always possible to conduct experiments in pairs. One experiment measures the readiness of black Americans to put considerations of race ahead of scores on achievement tests—the SAT experiment. We could do this once. We really couldn't do it twice.

So we have followed an additional strategy. Where appropriate we used measures from other studies. That means we not only asked about some of the same things but also asked about them in the same way. To be sure, our study mainly is about quite different things than previous studies of black Americans. They have concentrated on how blacks vote in presidential elections and what positions they take on issues of immediate relevance to black Americans—for example, whether government should work to improve the position of blacks. We concentrate on the readiness of blacks to embrace—or to reject—other Americans and their own identity as Americans. But despite the difference in focus, we made sure in advance that our study's results could be compared with those of other studies at a number of points. And just so far as the results of our study and those of previous studies are similar, and they are, that is another reason for confidence in our results.

From a specialist's point of view, statistical analysis is of value, not because it allows precise judgments about the way things are, but because it lets us gauge the imprecision of our judgments. From an intelligent, but not technically trained, reader's point of view, statistics may be worse than useless because they can make what otherwise would be readily comprehensible incomprehensible. From our point of view, there is no point to our having done what we have done if readers cannot immediately understand what we have done. So we say what we have to say as forcefully as we can and show what we have found as clearly as we can, while supplying in separate "sidebar" boxes the technical details specialists require.

Every study has limitations, ours very much included. But we believe this study opens to view aspects of the beliefs and commitments of African Americans that hitherto have been out of sight. So far as we have succeeded, we have many to thank. The National Science Foundation funded all of the surveys we rely on: the Black Belief Study (SBR-942016), the second Multi-Investigator Study (SBR-9633743), and the National Race and Politics Study (SES-8821575). In addition, the Achievement Based Award (SES-0111715) assisted completion of the writing of this book. There are not many social scientists who have had the opportunities to carry out original surveys of the American public that we have had. We are deeply grateful to the political science program at NSF and its director, Frank Scioli.

Needless to say, the NSF and the political science program are not responsible for the design of the study itself or the conclusions we have drawn from it. Nor are any of the many colleagues who have read drafts of this book and made sure that we did not lack for critical suggestions. These include: Henry E. Brady, Edward G. Carmines, Josh Cohen, Darren Davis, James Gibson, Martin Gilens, Donald L. Horowitz, Tamar Jacoby, James H. Kuklinski, Arthur Lupia, Diana Mutz, Philip Tetlock, and Alan Wolfe. We are grateful to all of them. We owe, however, a singular debt to Martin Shapiro. Every writer deserves a reader like Martin. Few get them. We are also heavily indebted to Eugenia Guilmartin for crucial help in preparing the figures and tables for this book. As for our editor, Chuck Myers, we would capsize if we took on board our full debt to him. He has been our colleague and has become our friend. We are also grateful for the assistance of the Survey Research Center and its director, Henry E. Brady, and of the Stanford Institute for the Quantitative Study of Society and its director, Norman Nie.

Now, at the end of this project, we want to remember a colleague who was with us at its beginning. Karen Garrett was the Manager of Survey Services at the Survey Research Center of the University of California, Berkeley, for 15 years. We worked side-by-side in the design of our studies. And, what is not to be forgotten, many young scholars got their first chance to do original research through the Multi-Investigator Surveys that Karen directed.

We cherish her memory.

BLACK PRIDE AND BLACK PREJUDICE

Sometimes separated by many years, sometimes by only a few, a succession of clashes—between blacks and Jews, blacks and Asians, blacks and Latinos, blacks and whites—have captured the headlines. There was, for instance, the Tawana Brawley case. It began with a false charge of sexual abuse by a young black woman against a group of police officers, then generated a series of ever more bizarre charges—against a Dutchess County, New York, assistant district attorney, and ultimately against the state attorney general and the governor of New York—with every allegation, however improbable, affirmed by prominent blacks.[1] There were the demonstrations against Freddy's Fashion Market, a Jewish-owned business in Harlem, protesting the failure to renew the lease of a black-owned business.[2] The demonstrators marched to the rhythm of anti-Semitic slogans and the demonstrations ended with the burning of the store and the murder of eight inside it.[3] There was the destruction of Korean-owned businesses in the Los Angeles riots. Their destruction—and the even more massive devastation of Latino-owned businesses—was variously explained or justified as a response to earlier mistreatment of black customers by Korean merchants.[4] And before all of these, there was the searing struggle in

[1] See McFadden, Blumenthal, Farber, Shipp, Strum, and Wolff 1990. The original charge was made in November, 1987.

[2] The decision not to renew the lease of the local black business was made by the building owner, a black church.

[3] The killings and fire took place on December 8, 1995. The event was covered extensively in the *New York Times* and other newspapers.

[4] For an uncommonly nuanced and revealing account that throws new light on the issue of intergroup conflict in potentially incendiary circumstances, see Lee 2002. The Los Angeles riots took place in April, 1992.

Ocean Hill-Brownsville in Brooklyn pitting black activists and a
black governing board against a teachers union led by a Jew and
made up disproportionately of Jews. Even after these many years,
Ocean Hill-Brownsville sticks in the minds of many Jews and blacks
as a symbol of the limits of the moral commitment of each to the
other.[5]

All these incidents, and many others as well, seem to teach a common lesson. There is first an explosive confrontation between blacks
and some other group, then a barrage of appeals for racial solidarity
by black activists to the larger black community, coupled with slurs
against the other group caught up in the confrontation, accompanied on occasion by the threat of violence and, sometimes, violence
itself. The lesson, it seems, is that appeals for black solidarity fuel
black intolerance and that black intolerance fuels appeals for black
solidarity.

Are black pride and black intolerance opposite sides of the same
coin? This question is at the center of this book.

I

We answer this question in the only way it can be
answered—by asking black Americans to share with us their thinking. From February to August in 1997, we talked to a representative
sample of black Americans in Chicago—756 in all.[6] We asked them
a great range of questions, from evaluations of prominent black
leaders such as Jesse Jackson and Louis Farrakhan, through their
views about core American values, to their views about a whole
variety of other groups in contemporary American society, among
them Jews, Asians, Latinos, and whites. We naturally inquired as to
their views about controversial issues like affirmative action, with
results that may surprise many. But we spent still more time
exploring their ideas about their sense of solidarity with other
blacks and their beliefs about the importance of blacks achieving
more control over their lives, greater recognition of black accom-

---

[5] See especially Ravitch 1974; see also Cannato 2001. The strike occurred in 1968.
[6] The Survey Research Center at the University of California, Berkeley, conducted
the interviews over the telephone. A technical description of the method of drawing
the sample and of its properties is set out in appendix A.

plishments, and a stronger sense of black pride and self-respect. And, though this may seem to turn things upside down, we asked to what extent are the values of black Americans the values of Americans as a whole?

It is of course natural to ask to what extent our findings may be generalized. Chicago, as both its partisans and critics will tell you, is unique in some respects, and black Chicagoans obviously may differ in some respects from black Americans who live in other cities, or who do not live in cities at all, or who live in quite different parts of the country. It is right to be concerned about whether blacks from Chicago are typical insofar as we picked Chicago precisely because it is atypical. It is the headquarters of Louis Farrakhan and the Black Muslims, and one of the aims of our study is to explore the impact of both on the thinking of black Americans. It surely is possible that blacks who live where Black Muslims are exceptionally prominent may be more committed to black pride and solidarity—or committed to a different conception of those ideals—than blacks who live elsewhere.

The problem of generalizability was a fundamental consideration in the design of our study. So we built in checkpoints, systematically incorporating questions from other studies of black Americans. This is particularly true for the measures at the center of our study, those of racial identification. The result is that we can compare our results with those of national surveys of black Americans, and see to what extent they are similar or not. But replication is only part of our effort. We also draw on a large-scale national survey of Americans that allows us directly to compare the views of black and white Americans.

But of course it is natural to ask a deeper question. How much trust can be put in public opinion surveys, quite apart from whether the respondents are black, white, or some other subset of Americans?

The objections to public opinion surveys are well rubbed, and they increasingly have been reinforced by the skepticism or cynicism (depending on your point of view) that has become so prominent a feature of American intellectual culture. For our part, let us put our cards on the table. First, there are limits to what can be learned from surveys. Second, given the crudity of measurement and the inherent abstractness of statistical analysis, the use of numbers can easily give a false sense of precision. Granting both points, the hand of the cynic is less strong than it seems. All forms of judgment, qualitative as well as quantitative, are imperfect. The whole point of the apparatus of quantitative studies—of representative sampling and systematic measurement—is not that it allows one to avoid error, but rather that it permits one to get an estimate of how much error there is.[7] More broadly, criticisms of the weaknesses of public opinion surveys remind us of Winston Churchill's sally in response to a question about the weaknesses of democracy. It is the worst form of government, he declared, except for all the others. So, too with public opinion surveys. Trying to infer what citizens think from the views of political activists or intellectuals, from the popularity of television shows or the sales of books or any other similarly indirect indicator of public opinion, is still worse. If you want to know what citizens think, it is necessary to ask them.

One can do this in the manner of a Studs Terkel, putting to each person the questions that seem most apt for him or her, following the twists and turns each conversation naturally and distinctively takes. Qualitative interviews can contribute much. But if you want to know what members of a large group—what citizens of a city or a state or a country characteristically think about some matter—it is necessary to carry out a public opinion survey. For all its limitations, and they are not trivial, the public opinion survey has the invaluable strength of representativeness. If you have picked the people you wish to interview in the proper way, it is possible to learn what is typically the case. And unless you know the way that things typically are, you have no way of telling whether any particular person you see or talk to represents the exception or the rule. What we want to map out is the landscape of opinion. That means identifying the points of view in the black community that command large amounts of support. Still more important, it means finding out how the views of black Americans about one subject most commonly fit together with their views about others, to form a larger, coherent outlook on life. There is no better way—indeed, no *other* way—to find this out than to carry out a properly representative survey of public opinion.

[7] So in reporting our results we will, when feasible, present both the absolute values that we observed and the confidence limits (or sampling errors) that should be placed around them.

II

This book is about a trio of questions. First, to what extent, and in what ways, do blacks in America take pride in being black? Second, what underlies an avowal of a racial identity—a sense of estrangement with America, a desire to be better-off personally, a need to compensate for feeling a lack of personal self-worth, or a lack of intellectual sophistication—or perhaps just the other way around, the very fact of being intellectually aware and engaged by the arguments of the day? Third, with what other ideas, beliefs about the world, assumptions about the nature of other people, is a sense of black identity and pride bound up—and, above all, to what extent is a feeling of racial identity and pride inclusive or, alternatively, chauvinistic in spirit?

Some of the answers to these questions are straightforward, or as nearly so as one might expect given the natural complexity of people's motivations. Others are more difficult, and what we have to contribute is correspondingly limited and tentative. The paramount question in gauging the meaning of black pride, however, can be put simply: If valuing being black means devaluing those who are not black, then black pride means one thing; if it does not, it means quite another.

One way we have tried to answer this question is to explore the relation between racial identification and anti-Semitism. How much anti-Semitism there is among black Americans—whether the level is higher, lower, or approximately the same as that among white Americans—is not our primary concern, though we appreciate that it is a question of wide interest. What is of consequence is whether there is a connection between being prejudiced and various ways in which blacks take pride in being black. If our findings are to be persuasive, they must be traced out in detail. What we can say here is that our results indicate that, with one important qualification, there is no connection between racial identification and black anti-Semitism.[8]

---

[8] As we shall show, other currents of contemporary black thought in addition to racial identification per se—among them, support for conspiratorial thinking and for Louis Farrakhan and the Black Muslims—do reinforce the susceptibility of black Americans to anti-Semitism.

The analysis of covariation—measuring what goes with what—is the standard approach in analyzing opinion surveys. But however esoteric the estimation technique, the limits of the standard approach are well known. In the stock adage, correlation is not causation. So we designed our study to exploit the strongest possible method—the randomized experiment.

We have carried out a whole battery of experiments specially designed to assess whether black loyalty and black intolerance really do go together. A specific illustration, however, may be worth mentioning. To see how racial identification may come into play in a conflict between blacks and Jews, we conducted the "College Editor" experiment. The design of the experiment is straightforward. One half of our respondents are asked whether a Jewish college editor who has published an article critical of black students should be fired. The other half are asked whether a black college editor who has published an article critical of Jewish students should be fired. Here, then, we have created a situation in which a conflict between Jews and blacks is presented in a mirror image form. In one case, it is a Jew who has done what blacks may take exception to; in the other, it is a black who has done exactly the same thing to Jews. Three points deserve emphasis. First, those who are asked about whether the Jewish editor should be fired cannot possibly figure out that the other half of the sample is being asked exactly the same question in reverse; and vice versa. Second, since the two halves are (chance differences aside) alike in every respect on account of experimental randomization, any difference in the way that our black respondents react *must* be because in one case the editor was Jewish and in the other a fellow black. Third, the College Editor experiment offers not one way but five to assess whether black pride feeds black intolerance: Are blacks more likely to favor firing a Jewish editor who criticized black students than a black editor who criticized Jewish students? Are blacks more likely to favor firing a Jewish editor the more strongly they identify themselves as blacks? Are they more likely to rally around a black editor and oppose firing him the more strongly they identify themselves as blacks? Are they more likely to favor firing a Jewish editor the more inclined they are to intolerance? And, not least interesting, are they more likely to rally around a black editor the more inclined they are to dislike Jews—in other words, does black prejudice reinforce black solidarity?

The answers to these questions illuminate in a way not possible previously the extent to which black pride encourages black intolerance. We shall state as unequivocally as possible what can be demonstrated for the first time thanks to the power of experimental randomization. First, taking pride in being black, when it makes a difference, leads blacks to be more likely to rally around a fellow black, but it does *not* lead them to be more likely to react against Jews. Second, being intolerant leads blacks to be more likely to reject Jews, but it does *not* in general lead them to be more likely to rally around a fellow black.

The relations between blacks and Jews, as symbolically and emotionally freighted as they are, are only one corner of our concern. We have carried out a battery of experiments centered on the relations between black Americans and a whole variety of other groups, including Asians, Latinos, whites, and even immigrants from Africa. Summarizing across these experiments, we will suggest that they point to two mirror-image conclusions. The first is this: On the one side, black pride encourages blacks to be more responsive to the needs and interests of fellow blacks, *but* on the other, it does not lead them to be more intolerant or punitive or hostile toward other groups in American society. Second, and conversely, black prejudice is not only largely independent of black pride, but it has just the opposite set of consequences. On the one side, black prejudice encourages blacks to reject others who are not black, while, on the other, it does *not* encourage them to identify with and rally around their fellow blacks. Quite the contrary: in certain circumstances, it can lead them to react negatively to fellow blacks.

III

One theme of this book is the sense of distinctiveness that black Americans feel by virtue of being black in America and the pride they take in a distinct black culture and identity. The other is the common ground, framework, and culture that black Americans, by virtue of being Americans, share with their fellow Americans.

What does a commitment to a common culture entail? It certainly does not require that black Americans agree with whites about whether race remains a serious problem in America, why black

Americans continue to find obstacles blocking their way forward, or
what the government should do about it. For perfectly obvious and
sensible reasons, black Americans tend to take a different view about
issues of race than white Americans do. A commitment to the common culture, however, means at least two quite specific and definite
things. The first is the repudiation of separatism. And our results on
this score are clear-cut. For black Americans who make up the heart
of the black community, separation as an end or as a means is overwhelmingly rejected. Indeed, our findings testify to the weight of
opinion among black Americans in favor of belonging to the larger
American society on the same terms as their fellow Americans: to
live and work alongside them, to strengthen the common culture
that binds them together, to cooperate and join together to achieve
a better society.

The second thing that a commitment to a common culture means
is hewing to a shared set of values. We acknowledge the difficulty of
truly gauging people's view of what should guide their lives, of the
ideals to which they believe they should strive to conform, of the
standards of conduct to which they conclude they should and must
adhere. This is a tricky business for all the obvious reasons, plus two
more. The first additional difficulty is that most of the values that
command support—freedom, the search for knowledge, order, the
claims of religion (in some version or other)—are of value to most
people. It follows that it is necessary to learn not whether black (or
white) Americans believe any or all of these are important—they
do—but something more complex: the balance they believe ought to
be struck between these values when one of them comes into conflict
with another. We attempt to gauge this balancing of conflicting values. Our approach is inevitably approximate, but we believe that our
findings on the similarity of values between black and white Americans are the more convincing just so far as they show that black and
white Americans do not simply value the same ideals, but strike
approximately the same balance among them when these values
come into conflict with one another.

The second difficulty in assessing values is that when people say
that they attach great importance to a particular value, how can we
tell that the value means the same thing to everyone? Take the
value of educational achievement. Suppose we were to ask repre-

sentative samples of black and white Americans whether they think
it is an important value. If they say that educational achievement is
an important value to them, there are the questions of how they
define such achievement, of the larger context in which they put it,
and therefore of the particular perspective from which they view it.
Black and white Americans may both be committed to achievement. Yet each may bring quite different background assumptions as
to what, given the fact of racial inequality in America, should be
taken as measures of it. Because we take seriously the possibility that
black and white Americans are committed to a common framework
of values, even to values like achievement that inescapably are
caught up in differences of opinion over the continuing place of race
in American life, we have worked to devise a challenging test of
whether there is a common commitment or not. We are thinking
particularly of the SAT experiment, which is described in chapter 4.
If you do not believe that black Americans are committed—win,
lose, or draw—to the larger American ideal of individual accomplishment after seeing the results of this experiment, nothing we
have done will persuade you.

In taking as one of our two principal themes the common ground
between black and white Americans, we do not at all mean to gain-
say the anger and frustration and bitterness that many blacks feel
about the persistence of racial inequality in America. That anger
toward, and conviction of, persisting injustice is one of the defining
features of contemporary black thought. Although it wells up in a
variety of ways, we shall pay particular attention to one—a susceptibility to conspiratorial thinking. The sense of the distance that
remains before equality becomes a reality, and the frustration and
anger it inspires, is real and important. But it is a profound error, we
have become persuaded, to allow this to obscure an even deeper
rootedness of black Americans as Americans.

Our two major themes—of distinctiveness and of inclusion—
may sound as though they are pulling in opposite directions. One
underlines the sense of difference blacks feel from other Americans,
especially white Americans; the other underscores their commonality with their fellow Americans, very much including white Americans. In some circumstances and for some people there is a strain
between the two themes. But we believe that an emphasis on the

potential for tension has obscured the bedrock character of black Americans' sense of themselves as Americans. For our findings show that, with only a minority of exceptions, black Americans can and do simultaneously affirm their distinctiveness as blacks and their commitment to the common culture they share with their fellow Americans.

We want to explore what it means when black Americans underscore their sense of having a racial identity, of feeling a sense of solidarity with fellow blacks. And the question of meaning is the issue. The ways in which black Americans can and do express a sense of racial identification, of racial solidarity, can differ, sometimes subtly, sometimes profoundly.

If you wish to learn what an idea signifies in politics, you cannot examine it in isolation. It is necessary to examine the ideas that accompany it, to establish, as it were, the company it keeps intellectually and socially. Part of what this process of inquiry involves is not difficult to see (which is not to say that it is easy to accomplish). We will have one sense of what it means for blacks to identify with being black, for example, if it is the case that blacks with the strongest sense of racial identification tend to have the weakest sense of self-worth. For if this is the case, it will be natural to interpret the appeal of racial solidarity in psychologically flavored self-therapeutic terms. On the other hand, if (as our findings suggest), blacks' view of racial solidarity and sense of self-worth have little of consequence to do with one another, we would be inclined to interpret the appeal of racial pride in quite different terms.

But if part of the task of unraveling what it means for black Americans to identify with being black in America is obvious, another part of it is not—even when, indeed especially when, the answers appear clear-cut. We have a very specific problem in mind. On the one side, as you will see, the idea of racial pride and identity has the strongest appeal to the most educated and best-informed blacks, and this is true however the notions of identity and solidarity are defined. This result suggests, obviously enough, that the ideas at the center of the appeal of racial solidarity are those of the best and the brightest. As will also be seen, however, ideas of racial identity are tied in the minds of black Americans to clusters of other ideas—about the achievements of ancient African civilizations and the ongoing occurrence of massive racial conspiracies—that on their face are so inflated and oversimplified as to invite rejection by critical minds. And yet the best educated and the most politically sophisticated blacks are just as likely to accept these exaggerations as the least educated or sophisticated—or even more so. How should these two lines of results be put together? That question occupies us in this chapter and throughout this study.

Forms of Racial Identification

The importance of black racial solidarity has been recognized since systematic research on the political beliefs of black Americans first got underway.[9] We are deeply indebted to this body of previous research, and have used it as a model for our own work at a number of specific points.[10] Nevertheless, our approach is different.

Previous work has presumed that there is one correct way to define the meaning of racial identification. The most obvious difficulty with this presumption is that, although everyone agrees that there is one core meaning, no one appears to agree what it is. In some work, the heart of the matter is a sense of "linked fate," a belief, that is, that what happens to you as a black in America is tied to what happens to other blacks in America.[11] In other work, the crux is a commitment to "black autonomy."[12] Writ large, the lesson is that "there are almost as many conceptualizations of black autonomy or solidarity," Welch, Bledsoe, Sigelman, and Combs remark,

[9] Among the many important studies that should be consulted are Gurin, Hatchett, and Jackson 1989; Tate 1993; Dawson 1994; and Allen, Dawson, and Brown 1989. For an original approach examining the intersection of race and residence coupled with exceptional clarity in analysis and presentation, see Welch, Sigelman, Bledsoe, and Combs 2001.

[10] We are especially indebted to Dawson 1994. We have used several measures developed in his study.

[11] Tate 1993.

[12] Dawson 1994.

"as there are researchers on the topic."[13] Moreover, the use of the different labels for the same measures, combined with the use of the same label for different measures, adds an additional pinch of confusion to a measurement recipe.[14]

A second difficulty is as obvious as the first. Since there are incestuously related ways of defining intimately related concepts, there is a danger of tautologically "explaining" one in terms of another. Suppose, for example, that you explain support for black nationalism or black autonomy in terms of whether blacks feel a sense of "linked fate" with other blacks.[15] On this view, because blacks believe that what happens to other blacks affects what happens to them, they are disposed to favor black nationalism or black autonomy. Someone else, however, can easily turn your explanation on its head. They can argue that just so far as blacks believe that blacks collectively should exercise a greater measure of control over their future, they will be inclined to believe that what happens to other blacks affects what happens to them. The problem is obvious. Ideas of black autonomy and linked fate are companion notions. Indeed, the truth of the matter is that they keep such close company that it is easy to argue that either one is the cause of the other. And since, from a conceptual standpoint, the two are so closely intertwined, which is causally responsible for the other cannot be empirically established.

A final difficulty is less obvious, but no less important. On everyone's results, ours as much as others', black Americans who embrace one aspect or expression of racial identity tend to embrace others. But because the same person embraces different ideas, it does not follow that they mean the same thing. Let us illustrate with an issue that goes to the core of our study: the relation, if any, between black pride and black anti-Semitism. As you will see, all of the aspects of racial identity and solidarity that we assess are related to anti-Semitism to some degree. Our conclusion is that this is mis-

[13] Welch, Sigelman, Bledsoe, and Combs 2001, chap. 5, fn. 3.

[14] For example, the measure that Allen and his colleagues label "black autonomy," Welch and hers label "racial solidarity," though the actual content of the latter measure is drawn from the former; while Dawson uses the same conceptual label, black autonomy, in both of his studies (1994, 2001), even though the content of the two measures is different.

[15] Dawson 2001 "explains" desiring black autonomy in terms of, among other things, feeling a sense of shared fate; see table A2.1, p. 333.

leading. Most of these forms of racial identification only appear to have something to do with it because they are related to Afrocentrism, which *is* genuinely connected to anti-Semitism. The point we want to make here is not that our claim about Afro-centrism and anti-Semitism is correct—depending on your view of the evidence we produce for it, you will find it persuasive or not—but that the very possibility of our laying out this case hinges on distinguishing different ways in which black Americans may take pride in being black. Combine them in a summary measure, or examine only one and neglect the others, and you foreclose the possibility of determining whether they may carry different charges. Hence our decision to explore a variety of aspects of racial identification.

Shared Fate

From an objective perspective, a person is a black American, a Jewish American, or an Irish American whether or not he or she acknowledges any sense of being black, Jewish, or Irish. But even if satisfying an objective criterion is a necessary condition of membership in a group, it is not ordinarily a sufficient one. It is hardly difficult, after all, to think of people who are Jewish by descent, but who do not think of themselves as Jewish in any degree. Accordingly, we usually feel that membership in a group calls for something more, that it requires some sense on the part of an individual that he regards himself of a member as a group.

But what does regarding or identifying yourself as a member of a group involve?[16] Most broadly, it entails a sense of sharing "common feelings, values, and interests."[17] But how can this general criterion of sharing "common feelings, values, and interests" be applied to

---

[16] See Miller, Gurin, Gurin, and Malanchuk 1981. In fact, this approach, which emphasizes not merely identification but "group consciousness," builds into the conceptualization of group relatedness a number of additional components, among them "polar power," or "expressed satisfaction or dissatisfaction with the group's current status, power, or material resources in relation to that of the outgroup" (Miller et al. 1981, p. 496). In our view, components additional to identification should be first shown to be empirically bound up with a sense of group attachment, and not incorporated into it as a matter of definition.

[17] Gurin 1985.

the particular question of whether black Americans have developed a sense of racial identification? Holding specifically which feelings, being committed to exactly which values, pursuing precisely what interests define being black in America? And since any feeling, interest, or value can be interpreted in multiple and often conflicting ways, why is one interpretation superior to every other?

It is indefensibly arbitrary to equate ex cathedra racial identification with only one possible interpretation of one set of possible values, feelings, and interests. So the established strategy has been to allow potential members of a group themselves to define whether they regard themselves as members of the group or not. This, too, can be done in different ways, but one way in particular has become standard: assessment of the degree to which one shares a sense of a common fate.[18] Just so far as you and they belong to the same group, and just so far as belonging to the group is of importance to you, then you should feel that what happens to other members of the group has a bearing on what happens to you. Accordingly, we asked all of our respondents:

How much do you think what happens to blacks in this country will affect your life—a lot, some, a little, or not at all?

Judged by the criterion of feeling that their fate is linked to the fate of fellow blacks, a large majority of black Americans manifestly feel a sense of racial identification. Approximately three quarters of them say that what happens to blacks in the country as a whole affects their lives somewhat, and, as can be seen in figure 2.1, almost two thirds of those say that it affects their lives a lot. Obviously, the precise numbers of blacks expressing a sense of shared fate will vary depending on the precise wording of the question, and equally obviously it also could make a difference whether the blacks who are interviewed are drawn from a particular city, as we have done, or from the country as a whole. But if our results are compared with those of other studies using different measures and different samples, the similarity is striking. By way of illustration, figure 2.1 also shows responses from the 1993–94 National Black Politics Study. There, two thirds say that their

[18] For example, Katherine Tate, who is closely associated with the criterion of "linked fate," has on occasion used as a criterion of racial group consciousness, in addition to a sense of sharing a common fate, the degree to which blacks think about being black; Tate 1991, p. 1166.

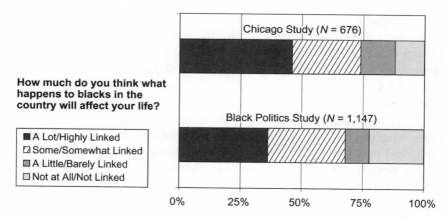

How much do you think what happens to blacks in the country will affect your life?

- ■ A Lot/Highly Linked
- ☑ Some/Somewhat Linked
- ■ A Little/Barely Linked
- □ Not at All/Not Linked

Figure 2.1. Share Common Fate

fate is linked to that of black people at least somewhat, and more than half of those say that it is "highly" linked.[19]

A Sense of Pride

A sense of common fate is one indicator of a sense of racial identification, but of course not the only indicator, nor even necessarily the most telling one. Another, nearly as obvious, is the importance attached to promoting a sense of pride among black Americans in being black. We wanted to put this issue of promoting black pride in the most natural terms. The common intuition is that choosing in favor of racial pride and solidarity comes, in some sense, at the expense of concord between races. We therefore asked all of our respondents:

> Is it more important for blacks to build good relations with whites or for blacks to build pride and respect for themselves, even if it means causing tension between blacks and whites?

[19] See Dawson 2001, table A1, pp. 327–33. It is worth observing that although Dawson's sampling frame is different from ours, his sampling strategy is the same, using a split sample design, with a subset of the sample being drawn through random-digit dial selection and a subset being drawn through list selection; see appendix A, "Sampling and Weighting," in the present volume.

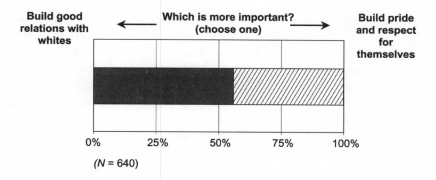

Figure 2.2. Build Black Pride

What they have to say is possibly not what you expected to hear. Given the choices of building good relations between blacks and whites or building black pride, 56 percent actually choose the former over the latter (figure 2.2). The division of opinion is surprisingly very close. Of course the two alternatives—building cross-racial ties and taking pride in being black—are not logically exclusive. It is possible to believe both. Indeed, we shall show that it is the rule that black Americans do believe both. Yet, the two sometimes can conflict, and the fact that a majority of black respondents choose in favor of building good relations with whites over strengthening black pride and self-respect points to a larger theme that we shall explore throughout this study—the ideal of common ground.

The Desire for Autonomy

We take the desire to strengthen black pride and self-respect to be one indicator of racial identification. But of course there are others, and black Americans who do not favor this one particular form of racial identification (perhaps because it is tied, in our question, to causing tension between blacks and whites) may very well favor others. For example, the desire of African Americans to exercise a greater measure of control over their economic lives is another way that the aspirations of black Americans to carve out a life in America *as African Americans* can express itself.[20] It would be sur-

[20] In taking a desire for black economic autonomy as one of several expressions of racial solidarity and pride, we are following, among others, Michael Dawson.

prising, given the history of American racism, if black Americans did not wish to have a larger say in the direction that their lives will take; still more surprising, if this wish for a larger say did not express itself in economic terms. How could it be otherwise? For all the genuine progress of the last forty years,[21] black Americans are more likely than white Americans to be impoverished; to live in decaying and squalid neighborhoods; to be unemployed or underemployed; to earn less (at any rate if they are male) and to own less, whether they are male or female.[22]

Two features of black Americans' desire for autonomy in general, and for economic autonomy in particular, need to be made clear at the beginning to avoid misunderstanding. First, some fantasists aside, the quest is not for absolute independence, but for a greater measure of it. Second, the goal is collective, not individual. The aim is not merely for individual blacks to make their way forward, but for blacks to advance as blacks. It follows that a paradigmatic expression of this desire for economic autonomy is the willingness of blacks to identify with and to support the economic enterprises of other blacks. Accordingly, we asked our respondents whether:

> Blacks should have control over the economy in mostly black communities.

We wanted to get a sense of the intensity, as well as of the direction, of opinion on this issue. Therefore, if respondents agreed with this idea of black control, they were invited to say whether they did so strongly or only somewhat; if they disagreed with it, they were invited to do the same.

How much support does the idea of economic autonomy enjoy in the black community? You might suppose that the idea of black control has become a political chestnut. Everyone in the black community accordingly would say that blacks should control the economy there. The only question would be how strongly they felt about black control of black businesses. The reality is more interesting. The balance of opinion does indeed favor black control of the economy in black communities. As figure 2.3 shows, 59 percent of our respondents agree that "blacks should have control over the econ-

[21] Jaynes and Williams 1989.
[22] Oliver and Shapiro 1995.

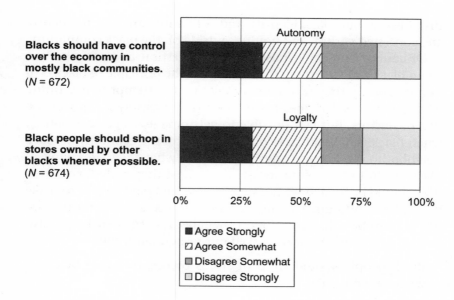

Blacks should have control over the economy in mostly black communities. (*N* = 672)

Black people should shop in stores owned by other blacks whenever possible. (*N* = 674)

Figure 2.3. Economic Autonomy

omy in mostly black communities," and of those who agree with the principle of black control, more than half do so strongly. But it is worth observing that a sizeable minority disagree—just over 40 percent—and almost half of those who do disagree do so strongly. Because of the way that the principle has been formulated, we ourselves are struck by the proportion of blacks who reject the principle of black control of the economy in black neighborhoods. In order that our findings could be compared to those of other studies, our question follows the wording of their question.[23] The established wording asks about black economic autonomy in isolation from any other consideration. No mention is made of any other principle with which it might conflict, nor of any cost that may possibly be incurred by implementing it—either or both of which increase rejection. Even so, a very large number of blacks reject it.

Our point is not that the desire for black control of businesses in black neighborhoods is not legitimate or consequential because blacks themselves disagree as to whether it is desirable. It is instead

[23] Dawson 2001.

that ideas about black identity and solidarity can, and frequently are, contested within, and not just outside of, the black community.

Of course, one could raise a deeper question and ask whether, when black Americans say that they favor the principle of black economic control, they mean what they say. To attempt to determine what people "really" mean is to enter (and possibly never leave) a hall of mirrors. But it is possible to get some leverage on whether, when blacks say that blacks ought to control the economy of black neighborhoods, there is anything behind what they are saying. If black control of black businesses is an ideal they truly favor, then they should be in favor of the steps they would have to take to make it a reality. And for black businesses to succeed as black businesses, blacks must be willing to support them because they are black businesses. Accordingly, we also asked our respondents whether:

> Black people should shop in stores owned by other blacks whenever possible.

As a glance at figure 2.3 will make plain, the division of opinion on black economic loyalty matches nearly exactly the division of opinion on black economic control. Again just under 60 percent agree that, whenever possible, blacks should buy from other blacks, and half of them do so strongly. And of course again, a sizeable minority disagree, and a majority of them do so strongly.

The responses to both questions, in their overall shape, are thus very nearly identical. This similarity is interesting but not directly to the point. For what we want to know is whether, to borrow an older language, if blacks will the end, they are prepared to will the means: if they say that they wish to have blacks control businesses in black neighborhoods, are they ready to back buying from black businesses themselves? Figure 2.4 provides a graphic answer. It provides a visual representation of the extent to which we can predict the position that blacks will take on shopping at black businesses given knowledge of the position they take on black control of businesses in black neighborhoods. To make the results transparent, we have projected a line showing how the position our respondents take on the principle of black economic autonomy (displayed on the horizontal axis) translates into the positions we predict they will take on shopping at black-owned businesses whenever possible (displayed on the vertical axis). The critical piece of information is the angle of the line: the steeper the slope, the more the position blacks

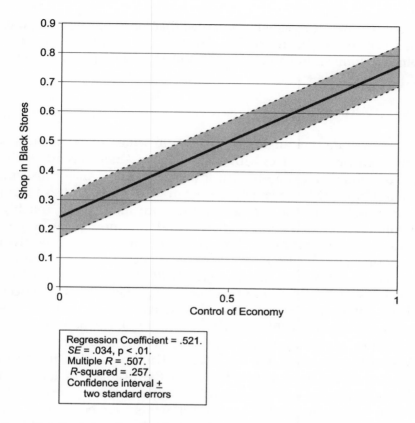

Figure 2.4. Predicting Shopping in Black Stores from Control of Economy

take on patronizing black businesses is tied to their views about black economic autonomy.[24]

The results could not be more clear-cut. What black Americans think about patronizing black businesses is very closely tied to what they think about blacks controlling the economy in black neighborhoods. If they favor one, they are very likely to favor the other; if they oppose one, they are very likely to oppose the other. Indeed, beliefs

---

[24] Here and throughout, the regression coefficients reported are unstandardized, in order not to confound the issue of the strength of association with the slope of the best-fitting line for a given pair of variables, and the variables are scored from 0 to 1. Thus, the result in figure 2.4 should be read as follows: a full one-unit change in views about black control of businesses in black neighborhoods—that is, a change from strongly disagree to strongly agree—is associated with a change of over half of the possible range (.521, to be exact) in readiness to patronize black businesses whenever possible.

about the two are so closely connected that for all practical purposes they can and will be treated as measures of the same thing and combined to form an Index of Support for Black Economic Autonomy.[25]

Afrocentrism

Yet another angle on the ways in which black Americans may identify themselves with being black in America is offered by the development of an Afrocentric perspective. For Americans who are not black, this is a largely unknown set of ideas, and so a word of explanation may be in order. By Afrocentrism, we mean, roughly, a commitment to a point of view aimed at honoring the accomplishments of African civilizations. Afrocentrism is manifestly a hard subject to represent in the right balance. Some work on the subject, for example, Martin Bernal's *Black Athena*, is based on much research, and even if that book's core claim that Egypt decisively influenced Greek civilization is seriously contested, it represents serious scholarship.[26] Our concern is with the popular representation of Afrocentrism, however. At this level, the core of Afrocentrism consists in a dual claim.[27] On the one side, it aims to show that claims made on behalf of the primacy of European accomplishments have been grossly exaggerated; on the other, that claims to genuine African accomplishments have been systematically slighted.

Both sides of Afrocentrism, the minimization of European civilization and the valorization of African civilization, lend themselves to claims that violate ordinary standards of evidence and reasoning. An example may be useful. Dr. Yosef A. A. ben-Jochannan, in the course of delivering the Martin Luther King, Jr. Memorial Lecture at Wellesley University, declared that Aristotle, while visiting Egypt, had "stolen his philosophy" from the library of Alexandria.[28] Since Aristotle died before the library in Alexandria was built, one would suppose Aristotle has an absolute defense against a charge of pla-

[25] The correlation between the two items is .51, and Cronbach's alpha for the Index of Black Economic Autonomy is .67.

[26] Lefkowitz and Rogers 1996. For a response, see Bernal 2001.

[27] See Howe 1998 and Walker 2001.

[28] We rely here on Mary Lefkowitz 1996, p. 2, writing as a member of the lecture audience.

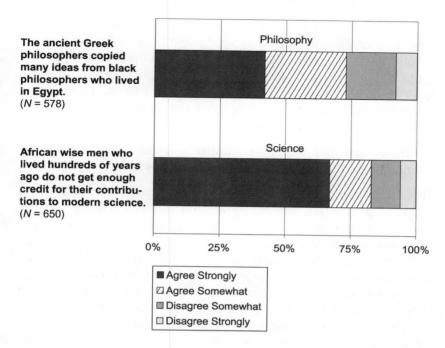

The ancient Greek philosophers copied many ideas from black philosophers who lived in Egypt.
(*N* = 578)

African wise men who lived hundreds of years ago do not get enough credit for their contributions to modern science.
(*N* = 650)

Figure 2.5. Afrocentrism

giarism of materials from it. But truth sometimes seems a secondary factor in the Afrocentric project. The primary considerations instead are symbolic and affective—most obviously, anger and resentment fueled by an insistence on black achievement. And the paramount objective is to put across a two-part assertion. First, signal achievements of mind and culture commonly credited to European civilization stem from the earlier civilization of Africa. Second, Europeans have improperly appropriated credit for these achievements, misleadingly presenting them as their own.

The combination of these two elements is potent in the contemporary black community. Consider our respondents' reactions when we asked whether they agree or disagree that:

> The ancient Greek philosophers copied many ideas from black philosophers who lived in Egypt.

Their response was one-sided. As the first bar of figure 2.5 shows, 73 percent agreed, and more than half of those did so strongly.

The emergence of philosophy was a keystone accomplishment of European civilization. Another keystone accomplishment was the development of science. Here, too, there is an opening for the core claim of Afrocentrism: that the crowning contributions of mind and culture began and took shape in African civilization long before European civilization materialized. We therefore asked our respondents whether they agree or disagree that:

African wise men who lived hundreds of years ago do not get enough credit for their contributions to modern science.

Their response, as figure 2.5 shows, is even more one-sided than before. Eighty-three percent agree that modern science has not acknowledged its debt to African wise men, and, of those who agree, eight in ten do so strongly.

To white Americans, these assertions may sound odd. But before one draws the wrong conclusion, he or she ought to consider a few examples of ideas in wide circulation among Americans generally. A Gallup poll from the late 1990s found that 71 percent of Americans thought the government was hiding something it knows about UFOs. Also, large numbers of Americans seem to believe that houses can be haunted and that extraterrestrials have visited the earth. For that matter, only a comparative handful believe that Lee Harvey Oswald acted alone in assassinating President Kennedy.[29] In short, large numbers of Americans, black or white, say things that appear odd or even off-the-wall, yet can make reasonable judgments about public affairs. Why not suppose that African Americans, in laying claims to the accomplishments of African wise men, are similarly giving off-the-cuff responses, yet can still come to grips with political reality?

Our answer, ultimately, will be that giving credence to the claims of Afrocentrism encourages a spirit of intolerance. For now, we would make the more limited point that in endorsing the claims of Afrocentrism, our respondents are expressing a definite point of view, not just giving off-the-cuff responses. Consider this test. If respondents are just offering superficial, top-of-the-head responses, then how they respond to one of these statements should not have

[29] We are indebted to Martin Gilens both for the general point and the specific examples.

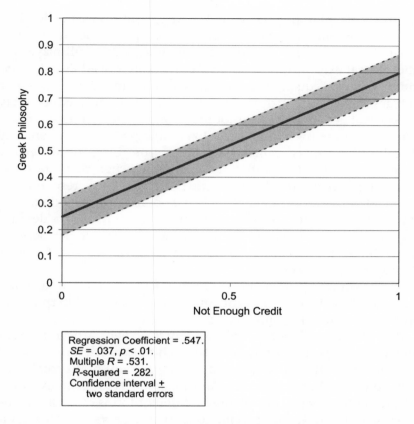

Figure 2.6. Predicting Greeks Copied Ideas from Not Enough Credit

very much to do with how they respond to the other. On the other hand, if they have formed a definite view on Afrocentrism, then how they respond to one should be bound up with how they respond to the other. Indeed, the more definite and coherent their view on Afrocentrism, the better able we should be to predict how they respond to one of these statements by knowing how they have responded to the other.

Just as we looked at the connection between ideas about economic autonomy for blacks, we look at the connection between ideas about Afrocentrism (figure 2.6). Again we project a line showing how the position our respondents take on modern science failing to acknowledge the contribution of African wise men (displayed on the horizontal axis) translates into the positions we predict they will take on whether ancient Greek philosophers copied many of their ideas from black philosophers who lived in Egypt (displayed on the vertical axis). And just as we saw a steeply sloped line the first time, we see an equally steep line this second time. This means that if blacks agree that "African wise men who lived hundreds of years ago do not get enough credit for their contributions to modern science," they are overwhelmingly likely to agree that "the ancient Greek philosophers copied many ideas from black philosophers who lived in Egypt." If they disagree with either, they are overwhelmingly likely to disagree with the other. Since responses to one statement are so closely tied to responses to the other, it is appropriate to infer that black Americans have formed a definite stance toward the ideas at the core of an Afrocentric perspective. Accordingly we combine responses to the two items to form an Index of Afrocentrism.[30]

Granted that black Americans have a definite, coherent attitude toward the claims of Afrocentrism, how should we interpret the quite overwhelming support they express for claims about the indebtedness of science and philosophy to ancient African civilizations? Our responsibility is to try to catch hold of what they meant in making a particular assertion by taking account of the totality of what they said in the interview. And a first step is to get an overview of the connections, if any, between different forms of racial identification. Obviously, the specific form they take varies. There is a sense of sharing a common fate, of believing that what happens to other blacks bears on what happens to you as a black; that it is important to build black pride and self-respect; that economic autonomy for blacks is an important goal to achieve; and that the achievements of blacks—even of ancient African civilizations—ought to be acknowledged. But just so far as they all represent ways for black Americans to express an identification with being black, then those who affirm one way should affirm the others. And just so far as this is true, knowing how people feel about one of these idea-elements should allow one to predict how they feel about any other.

All of these idea-elements tend to go together, some very closely, as we see in table 2.1. Blacks favoring economic autonomy are markedly

---

[30] The correlation between the two items is .53, and Cronbach's alpha is .69.

TABLE 2.1
Consistency between Various Black Attitudes
(Correlation Coefficients)

	Autonomy	Afrocentrism	Common Fate	Build Pride
Autonomy	1.00			
Afrocentrism	.46	1.00		
Common Fate	.36	.36	1.00	
Build Pride	.37	.31	.24	1.00

Note: Minimum $N = 532$; all $p < .01$.

more likely to embrace an Afrocentric perspective, and those who
share a sense of common fate are markedly more likely both to favor
economic autonomy and embrace an Afrocentric perspective. The
only exception to this pattern of strong interconnections is a somewhat weaker link between sharing a sense of common fate and wanting to build black pride. Each of them, however, is strongly tied to the
other three elements. And because they manifestly have something in
common, it is reasonable to treat each as a way for black Americans to
express a sense of identification with being black.

But to say that these different ways of expressing a racial identification have something in common is not to say that they are the
same thing. On the contrary, as we made our way through the
process of analyzing our data, we came across important points of
difference between these various forms of racial identification. So in
setting out our results we shall proceed in a way that allows both
their points of similarity and of difference to be visible.

We shall begin by exploring what lies psychologically behind
black Americans' feeling a sense of distinctiveness as black Americans. More particularly, we shall take a look at an idea that has
gained considerable currency: that what drives the campaign to recognize publicly the worth of minorities is their need to establish a
sense of personal worth.

The Politics of Self-Esteem

A generation ago, there was an optimism about the ease
with which people could cross boundaries between groups. Equally,

there was an innocence about their desire to do so. But informed opinion has changed. It no longer is taken for granted that a sense of difference is a bad thing. On the contrary, it has become common to argue that a sense of difference is a good thing, especially for those traditionally stigmatized as different.

"White society," the leading theorist of difference, Charles Taylor, has declared, "has for generations projected a demeaning image of [blacks], which some of them have been unable to resist adopting. Their own self-depreciation, on this view, becomes one of the most potent instruments of their own oppression."[31] Why oppression? Because African Americans' sense of who they are and what they are worth is limited by the larger society's sense of who they are and what they are worth. On this view, members of subordinate groups see themselves not as they actually are, but rather as they appear to be, reflected in the images that members of the superordinate group hold of them. And if the superordinate group does not place a high value on them, they will place a low value on themselves.

But this very source of oppression, Taylor insists, can be a source of liberation. If the larger society can be induced to place a higher value on a minority group, then the sense of self-worth of minorities can be heightened. Hence the potentially redemptive function of the politics of black pride. By insisting that the larger society recognize the worth of the distinctive contributions of blacks, blacks themselves will be more likely to recognize their own worth. Societal standing thus becomes the key to self-realization.

This quest for status and self-realization may sound innocuous, even banal, in a culture that has come to celebrate the psychology of self-esteem. And the intentions that underlie Taylor's argument for campaigns to acknowledge the historic accomplishments of blacks (and other minorities) are compassionate, even if much in the actual campaigning has proven to be self-serving. He wishes blacks to be not merely better off materially, economically, but to become more fully what they genuinely are capable of becoming. Yet the implications of Taylor's argument are, ironically, both self-limiting and patronizing.

Most obviously, there is the irony of winning freedom for a group from the larger society at the cost of losing it within the group

[31] Taylor 1994, p. 26.

itself. Isaiah Berlin has pungently discussed this problem, and his words are worth quoting in full:

> I may feel unfree in the sense of not being recognized as a self-governing individual human being; but I may feel it also as a member of an unrecognized or insufficiently respected group: then I wish for the emancipation of my entire class, or community, or nation, or race. . . . So much can I desire this, that I may, in my bitter longing for status, prefer to be bullied and misgoverned by some member of my own race or social class, by whom I am, nevertheless, recognized as a man and a rival—that is as an equal—to being well and tolerantly treated by someone from some higher and remoter group, who does not recognize me for what I wish to feel myself to be.[32]

Berlin's warning applies across the board, not to blacks either exclusively or distinctively. But it does apply to them directly. It is not, after all, hard to recount examples of black leaders who have ill-served their black constituents, yet maintained their grip on political power through appeals for racial solidarity.

Other implications of Taylor's insistence on the importance of recognition are perhaps less obvious. The idea of compensatory gain, the notion, that is, that a subordinate group will place a higher value on itself if the superordinate group places a higher value on it, has an intuitive appeal. Surely it is understandable that the inferior status to which blacks were condemned—indeed, the judgment of the larger society that they were inferior—must have left a mark, must have left blacks with a sense that they are inferior. And surely it follows that if blacks (or other minorities) come to value more highly the accomplishments of their group, they will come to value themselves more highly in the bargain.

But if the argument for a politics of recognition is meant to be a compassionate one, it nonetheless is a patronizing one. It presumes that African Americans are psychologically damaged—that they agree that they are inferior to white Americans. The evidence for this, one can say at a minimum, is very far from conclusive.[33]

---

[32] Berlin 1969, p. 157.

[33] From this angle, the argument over the politics of recognition is a contemporary variation of a classic liberal argument on the wounds blacks have suffered as a consequence of discrimination. This theme is expertly developed by Scott 1997.

Still more important, the argument for recognition presupposes that black Americans cannot build a sense of their individual worth on the basis of their actual accomplishments in their own lives, in the success that they achieve in personal relations, at work, in school, or in the activities of life that they value. The argument instead is that if blacks (and other minorities) are to appreciate their true value, it is necessary that the true value of the contributions of blacks (and other minorities) be recognized. But recognized by whom? Crucially, in Taylor's view, recognized not only by blacks; indeed, not even primarily by blacks. From his perspective, the whole point behind insisting on a public acknowledgment of the accomplishments of blacks is to ensure that those who are not black acknowledge the accomplishments of those who are black.

It would be nice if white Americans acknowledged the achievements of black Americans; certainly, it would be appropriate. But why is it necessary? Because, according to Taylor, it is not within the power of subordinate groups to bestow on themselves a full sense of their own self-worth. For a subordinate group to recognize its worth, the superordinate group must acknowledge it. So for black Americans to appreciate their own achievements, it is necessary that white Americans acknowledge what blacks have achieved. The argument on behalf of a campaign for black pride in order to bolster black self-esteem thus rests on the patronizing presumption that blacks remain fundamentally dependent on whites for their sense of their worth as blacks.

Because an idea is patronizing, it does not follow that it is false. Many distasteful ideas are true. It is possible that blacks feel they are inferior to whites. And it is possible that they can be persuaded that they are capable of achievement if whites praise what blacks have achieved. But although both are logically possible, in our judgment neither is empirically probable. On the evidence of systematic studies, black Americans do not suffer a lack of self-respect or a damaged sense of identity or a shrunken sense of self-esteem.[34] Moreover, the lesson learned from systematic studies of self-esteem is that indi-

---

[34] For the most recent and comprehensive review of research and ambitious empirical analysis, see Allen 2001. For his specific judgment on comparative levels of self-esteem for black and for white Americans, see ibid., p. 61.

viduals, whether black or white, are likely to have a stronger sense of self-worth and personal competence just so far as they have a history of actual accomplishment. And for black Americans just as for white, the recognition that brings their accomplishments home to them comes from those they actually live with—the people they work alongside, go to school with, or against whom they directly compete—not from some abstract valuation in the larger society.[35]

But what is a different matter is whether the movement on behalf of racial pride owes its appeal, in some significant measure, to the balm it promises for a wounded sense of self-worth. Perhaps because of the way that white America historically has stigmatized blacks, they owe a greater measure of their personal sense of self-worth to the sense of worth that the larger society accords them. And if so, then perhaps one of the appeals of taking pride in being black is that it helps blacks bolster their sense of personal worth.

Our study includes a measure of self-esteem taken from the California Psychological Inventory (CPI), one of the most widely used instruments for measuring normal personality. It is worth observing that the measurement strategy behind the CPI is to select items to assess a psychological attribute, not on the basis of expressly referring to the attribute, but purely on the basis of their empirical power to discriminate between individuals who independently have been shown to have a high degree or a low degree of the target attribute. This, it is worth noting, makes CPI measures less vulnerable to impression management. Drawing on the archives of the Institute for Personality and Social Research at the University of California, Berkeley, a short-form measure of self-esteem was developed through detailed item analyses of the measure of self-acceptance.[36]

If you look at the results in table 2.2, you will see that the value that blacks place on themselves as individuals and the value they place on being black have little to do with each other. Thus, the importance that they attach to the notion that blacks should "build pride and respect for themselves" has nothing to do with whether their own level of self-esteem is high or low. And the same is true for sharing a sense of common fate. Blacks who feel that what happens

---

[35] See especially Rosenberg and Simmons 1971.

[36] We want to thank Pamela Bradley for the analyses on which item selection was based. The specific wording of all the questionnaire items is set out in appendix B.

TABLE 2.2
Self-Esteem and Racial Identification
(Correlations with Self-Esteem Measure)

	Racial Identification Measure			
	Autonomy	Afrocentrism	Common Fate	Build Pride
Chicago Study	.13*	.09*	.06	.01
Allen Study	.14	.15	–	–

Note: Minimum Chicago $N = 562$; *$p < .05$.

to blacks in the country as a whole greatly affects what happens to them are not significantly more likely to have higher or lower levels of self-esteem than blacks who believe that what happens to other blacks has no impact on what happens to them. There is a modest relation between self-esteem and support for economic autonomy, as there is also for Afrocentrism. The more black respondents support black autonomy and Afrocentrism, the higher their level of self-esteem.

For purpose of comparison, we include results from Richard Allen's recent study on the black self-concept.[37] Allen's focus is the psychology, rather than the politics, of racial identification, but at a few points his results and ours can be put alongside each other. The comparison between the two studies is particularly interesting since Allen's study is based on a sample of black Americans from Detroit while ours is based on a sample from Chicago. The comparison also is potentially risky because some of his measures—particularly his measures of self-esteem and of African self-consciousness—are different from ours. It therefore would not be surprising if his results differed from ours. Yet his measure of self-esteem is the best documented of measures of self-regard, and his other measures have been carefully developed.

The bottom row of table 2.2 compares the findings of Allen's study and ours, showing the correlations between his measure of self-esteem, on the one side, and his measures of support for black autonomy and African self-consciousness, on the other. As you can see, the relations are similarly modest to those in our study. Indeed,

[37] Allen 2001, table 6.3, p. 154.

the numbers are virtually identical. Again the suggestion is that the more our black respondents support black autonomy and an African identity, the higher their level of self-esteem, though again the strength of these relations must not be exaggerated.

Credulousness or Sophistication?

A sense of racial identification, whatever the specific form we have canvassed, is widespread in the black community. But it is by no means universal. How has this set of ideas about the importance of pride and the recognition of black accomplishment and a feeling of solidarity made its way through the black community?

There are two off-the-rack accounts of the diffusion of ideas. The focus of the first is credulousness. Having only a thin fund of information to draw on, or lacking the skills and habits of critical judgment, leaves people susceptible to persuasion: and just so far as they are more readily persuasible in general, they are more easily persuaded to identify themselves with a new social or political movement, perhaps particularly if it infuses their lives with a sense of meaning and purpose.[38] On this view, the appeals of racial identification should be stronger the less well informed or sophisticated blacks are. According to the second view, however, things are exactly the other way around. New ideas find their audience, not among the least well informed and the least intellectually sophisticated, but among the most, because it is the most intellectually engaged who are the most likely to be exposed to and aware of new ideas.[39] Depending on circumstance, both accounts—the one centered on credulousness, the other on sophistication—can apply. The question is, which offers a key to the appeals of racial identity and solidarity?

It must be acknowledged that the hypothesis of credulousness has an intuitive plausibility. Part of the history of blacks in America is a chronicle of charismatic figures preaching a fantasized version of the history of blacks, sometimes in expressly religious terms, as with Elijah Muhammad, sometimes in overtly secular ones, as with Marcus Garvey. Moreover, historical precedents aside, some contempo-

[38] The classic presentation of this argument on cognitive simplism and education is Selznick and Steinberg 1969.

[39] Zaller 1992.

rary expressions of racial identification suggest the lure of the fabu-
lous. But we could as easily cite the enormous receptivity we have
observed to core claims of Afrocentrism. Consider the claim that
modern science has not acknowledged its debt to African wise men.
Examined clinically, it seems a specimen type of the combination of
fantasy and simplification that enjoys its greatest appeal among
those whose skills of critical judgment are weakest.

How is it possible to tell whether black pride trades on gullibility?
There are two standard measures of intellectual sophistication in the
study of public opinion. One is the breadth of a person's intellectual
horizons and cognitive skills as measured by years of formal education. The other is the level of his or her political sophistication as
measured by a battery of questions about politics and political institutions.[40] As a first approximation, this suggests a test. If the appeal
to racial solidarity and race pride does capitalize on gullibility, the
least well educated and the least politically sophisticated blacks
should be the most likely to have strong racial identifications.

But this is only a first approximation. Racial identification can
take different forms, and depending on which form of identification
you have in mind, different arguments can be mounted about how
they may be related to intellectual sophistication. Consider the
sense of sharing a common fate. For the first time, there is a substantial black middle class, and the more important that you think
that class differences among blacks have become, the less you are
likely to expect that middle-class blacks will believe that what happens to blacks *in general* makes a difference to what happens to
them. On the other hand, surely it is just as plausible that feeling a
sense of common fate leads you to see connections between the
larger world of affairs and your immediate circumstances. And part
of the point of being intellectually sophisticated is precisely that it
allows you to see connections of this order—in seeing that what
happens to other blacks may have something to do with what happens to oneself.

---

[40] Specifically, which political party has the most members in the House of Representatives in Washington; how much of a majority is required in the U.S. Senate and
the House of Representatives to override a presidential veto; which party, the Democratic or the Republican, is the more conservative; and whose responsibility it is—the
president's, Congress's, or the Supreme Court's—to determine if a law is constitutional
or not.

TABLE 2.3
Correlations between Education, Political Information, and Racial
Identification
(Correlation Coefficients)

	Education	Political Information
Racial Identification		
Autonomy	.17	.26
Afrocentrism	.28	.16
Common Fate	.10	.14
Build Pride	.13	.18

Note: Minimum $N = 552$; all $p < .05$.

There are thus grounds for expecting that identifying with being
black will go along with being less intellectually sophisticated, and
grounds for expecting that it will go along with being more so. To
tell which is right, we have plotted the relation between belief in a
common fate and both blacks' level of education and political information. If gullibility is the key, then the lower our black respondents' level of education or political information, the stronger
should be their sense that what happens to other blacks has something to do with what happens to them; that is, the direction of the
relationship between the two should be negative. In fact, the result
is *exactly opposite*. The relationship between both education and
political information on the one hand, and feeling a sense of common fate, is positive rather than negative, as you can see from the
fact that, in table 2.3, the signs of both coefficients are positive, not
negative. That is, the more formal schooling our black respondents
have had, and the more extensive their knowledge of politics, the
more (not the less) likely they are to believe that what happens to
other blacks has an effect on their lives.

Nor is this result aberrant. Consider the relation between wishing
to build black pride and intellectual sophistication. Again it is the
most politically sophisticated and best-educated blacks, not the
least, who are the most likely to believe that it is important for
blacks to build pride and respect for themselves. And the same holds
for support for black economic autonomy. Again it is the most
politically aware and best-educated blacks, not the least, who are the
most likely to believe that blacks should control the economy in

black neighborhoods and that blacks should buy from black-owned businesses whenever possible. The relations vary in strength, from modest to more substantial, depending on the particular aspect of racial identification and whether it is political awareness or education at which we are looking. What is impressive, though, is their consistency. If credulousness or gullibility were the source underlying black pride, then the relation between intellectual sophistication (however it happens to be measured) and racial identification (however it happens to be measured) would be negative. But not only is this not the case, it is always just the other way around. It is the more politically aware and the better educated, not the less, who are more likely to feel a sense of common fate, to want to build black pride, and to support black economic autonomy. Intellectual awareness and political engagement, not gullibility or credulousness, is the key to black pride.

Ideas of black affirmation, of the value of black solidarity, of the need to develop a stronger sense of pride in being black—all are now prominent in the public rhetoric of virtually every well-known black leader. They are ideas that are in circulation in the black community, both through black organizations and black media. And it is the most educated and politically sophisticated segments of the public who are the most likely to embrace the ideas that are in vogue. They are the most likely, because they are the ones most likely to be exposed to ideas as they circulate through a community, to comprehend them, and to see their relevance to their own lives. This pattern of diffusion of ideas has nothing to do with race, even though racial identification is what is at issue here. For black and white alike, part of what it means to be intellectually sophisticated and engaged is to participate in the current of ideas that circulate through a community at any given moment.

But does this rule apply absolutely across the board, without any exception whatever? We have so far talked about three forms of racial identification: feeling a sense of common fate with other blacks; wanting to build black pride; and desiring to increase the autonomy of blacks. What about when racial identification takes a more disputable form, as in the case of Afrocentrism?

Think of the pair of tenets of Afrocentrism we have considered. One is that modern science owes an unacknowledged debt to African wise men. The other is that ancient Greek philosophers copied many of their ideas from African predecessors. Both of these claims violate standard canons of plausibility. And both do so conspicuously. Each is the kind of oversimplified statement that the intellectually sophisticated ordinarily are on guard against and normally take as grounds, if not for rejection, then at a minimum for caution. Surely, the most intellectually sophisticated blacks—those who have had the fullest benefit of education and are the most politically aware—should be at least somewhat more reluctant to endorse them than the least intellectually sophisticated blacks. Yet, as table 2.3 also shows, it is the most educated blacks, the most politically aware blacks, not the least, who are the most likely to endorse the claims of Afrocentrism.

This seems a paradox. The more critically intelligent blacks are, the more publicly credulous they appear to be. But the beliefs and feelings of blacks need to be viewed against the background of their singular historical experiences. These particular claims for acknowledgment of black accomplishments are oversimplified. But there *is* an issue of acknowledgment. Blacks have made important contributions to American history, culture, and institutions. It could be said that the contributions of blacks were airbrushed out of standard accounts of American history except that this formulation is too anodyne. It slights the active resistance to acknowledging the contributions of black Americans that, until recently, has dominated the memorializing of the American experience. Against a background of blindness and bias, it does not seem implausible to suggest that the allegation at the heart of Afrocentrism—the charge of cultural theft—carries a twofold message. In the first place, Afrocentrism represents, if you will, an allegorical way to call attention to injustices done to blacks in general and disparagement of their intellectual contributions in particular. And, in the second place, Afrocentrism has a retributive function. It is not just an assertion that things are wrong. It is a demand that they be put right. And so far as what is involved is this two-part message—acknowledging the wrongs and putting them right—the appearance of paradox dissolves. Afrocentrism is—in part—one more way of demanding that the status of black Americans be improved, and more sophisticated blacks are more likely to back this demand for the same reasons that they are more likely to back other appeals for racial solidarity.

But the diffusion of ideas in vogue to those most exposed to ideas in general is only a part of the story. There is also the question of who benefits. To what extent are political ideas like racial pride and affirmation in vogue now because their adoption brings personal—that is, economic—benefits?

Racial Affirmation and Self-interest

We have found that the more educated and the more politically aware that blacks are, the more likely they are to express a gamut of manifestations of black pride. We have interpreted this finding as indicating that the most intellectually sophisticated tend to be the most likely to pick up the ideas in circulation at any given moment. But a different interpretation is possible. Since the best educated and the most politically informed also tend to be the best-off, perhaps it is not really education or political engagement that matters. Perhaps it is instead self-interest.

On a self-interest interpretation, blacks who are most likely to benefit from the development of black businesses are the most likely to support black economic autonomy. Similarly, blacks who are the most supportive of efforts to win recognition of black accomplishments are those who are most likely to benefit from campaigns to acknowledge black achievement. They favor these ideas in both cases because it pays off to favor them. And in speaking of a payoff, proponents of a self-interest interpretation have in mind that blacks rally around the banner of black pride because it pays them personally, individually, to do so, not because it benefits blacks in general if they do so.

It may sound cynical to suggest that blacks express racial loyalty based on a calculus of personal advantage. But this intuition lies behind a quite general account of group identification, having nothing to do with race itself. By contrast with a traditional perspective, in which the sources of group identification and loyalty are seen as diffuse, social, and emotional, in this new perspective the appeals of group solidarity and pride are individual, material, and rational.[41] Individuals identify with groups—they see themselves as blacks or Serbians or French, and feel a sense of solidarity and pride in their

---

[41] Hardin 1995 is the classic text setting out this view.

group identity—because they wish to be better-off as individuals.[42] It's a matter of what's in it for them.

This view of group loyalty in some sense may be cynical, but in no sense is it nihilistic. On a self-interest account, group loyalties are not just masks donned insincerely. They represent genuine commitments. But in interpreting the connection between group loyalty and personal advantage, which is cause and which effect is crucial. On a traditional account, we come to have an interest in a group doing well because we have come to value it. On a self-interest account, we come to value a group because we have an interest in *ourselves* doing well.[43]

From a self-interest perspective, the crucial word in characterizing the black pride movement as a middle-class movement—that is, as a movement disproportionately supported by better educated and better-off blacks—is "class." Middle-class blacks *are* more likely to favor more businesses being owned by blacks and to favor blacks pledging to buy from black-owned businesses wherever possible. And on a self-interest interpretation they are more likely to do so because, by virtue of being middle-class, they are the ones who will own these businesses. Or to put the point more broadly, middle-class blacks are more likely to favor identity politics because they are more likely to get the better jobs, the greater gains in income, the larger jump in status that has followed in the wake of racial affirmation and affirmative action.

The possibility that black Americans identify themselves as black in America (at least in part) because it pays to do so cannot be dismissed out of hand. But racial identification can take a variety of forms. The idea that blacks should buy from black businesses or that blacks should control the economy in black neighborhoods is just one way for blacks to express their racial identity and sense of solidarity with other blacks. Another way, as we have seen, is to insist on the acknowledgment of the achievements of ancient African civilizations. But if it is not hard to see how middle-class blacks can profit from more business opportunities for black businessmen, it is not immediately obvious how charging ancient Greek philosophers with plagiarism or modern science with a failure to acknowledge the

[42] Hardin 1995, p. 67
[43] Hardin 1995, p. 64.

contributions of African wise men will bring material benefits to modern black Americans.

One could reply that the benefits follow from racial solidarity in general, and that any specific sign of solidarity can serve the purpose as well as any other. Yet, surely it is necessary to go on and ask, why *this* sign of solidarity? We have seen that well-educated, middle-class blacks are distinctively likely not only to support more opportunities for black business, but also more likely to endorse the tenets of Afrocentrism. Why the latter as well as the former?

The answer, according to Manning Marable, follows from the connection between class and status. Who should be more receptive than the black middle class, he asks, to the claim that blacks have a unique history of achievement that now must be recognized, and rewarded? "[V]ulgar Afrocentrism," he writes, "was the perfect social theory for the upwardly mobile black petty bourgeoisie. It gave them a vague sense of ethnic superiority and cultural originality, without requiring the hard, critical study of historical realities."[44]

This is a provocative claim. It amounts to asserting that African Americans adopt forms of racial identification like Afrocentrism as a status badge. And if this is true for Afrocentrism, why should it not be true, at least in part, for other forms of racial identification? But Marable's argument about the importance of status, and the broader claim about the importance of economic benefits, are just claims. They may be true. Or they may be false. The all-important question is whether the evidence shows them to be true.

If the mainspring of support for black pride and black solidarity is gaining more economic benefits or enjoying higher social status, then the better-off blacks are, the stronger will be their racial identification. As a first approximation, figure 2.7 plots the extent to which support for the various forms of racial identification that we have surveyed—promoting black economic autonomy, building black pride, feeling a sense of common fate, Afrocentrism—increases as income increases.[45] The angle of the regression line indicates the extent to which the appeal of various forms of racial identification is tied to income: the steeper the slope, the more pronounced the connection.

[44] Quoted by Howe 1998, p. 281.
[45] One hundred fifty-six respondents declined to answer the income question.

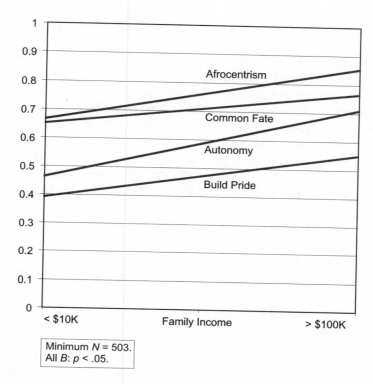

Figure 2.7. Predicting Racial Identification from Family Income (Regression Lines)

In every case, the higher blacks' family income, the greater the appeal of racial identity and solidarity. The relation is not equally strong in every case, but it is statistically significant in all. Should we conclude, therefore, that support for greater economic autonomy for blacks, or for more recognition of the accomplishments of blacks, or for racial solidarity in general is in a significant degree self-serving? Does the evidence we have seen demonstrate that the forms of racial solidarity and identity owe their appeal to a desire, consciously recognized or not, either to be better-off materially or to enjoy more status socially?

The answer may be yes, but on the evidence to this point it is not necessarily so. If all we know is that having more money tends to go along with having stronger racial identifications, we can't tell whether the relation between them points to the importance of class (whether in the sense of being better-off materially or enjoying higher status socially) or of intellectual sophistication, since people who are better-off tend also to be better educated, and vice versa. Moreover, this particular indeterminacy—is it education or is it class?—is just an example of a broader set of problems. Earlier we saw that there is a positive relation between our black respondents' levels of self-esteem and their support for at least some forms of racial identification. But people, black or white, who are better-off and better educated tend to have higher self-esteem than those who have less money and are poorly educated.[46] But then we may observe a correlation between taking pride in being black and higher self-esteem only because higher self-esteem goes along with higher education and higher incomes.

A way to resolve this uncertainty is to look at the connection between racial identification and all of these factors simultaneously rather than one at a time. Look first at the results for Afrocentrism (first column of table 2.4). As you will see, education makes a difference. The more educated our black respondents are, the more likely they are to endorse Afrocentric sentiments. But while education makes a significant difference, both income and self-esteem do not. They only appeared to be related to Afrocentrism because each of them is also related to education. The same applies to feeling a sense of common fate. Again education makes a difference—the more educated our black respondents are, the more likely they are to share a sense of common fate with other blacks. And again income and self-esteem are irrelevant.

Indeed, through all of the forms of racial identification the common strand is education. The more formal schooling our black respondents have had, the more likely they are to identify themselves as black and to take pride in this identification. But there are two additional aspects of the results to note. The first is this: Income as well as education is a significant predictor of black support for black economic autonomy. This is the only time that income matters when it comes to the likelihood of blacks identifying themselves as blacks, and it pays to be prudent about putting a lot of weight on exceptions. But it is intriguing to observe that the only aspect of

[46] In our study, the correlations between our measure of self-esteem and of education and income are .31 and .28, respectively.

TABLE 2.4

Predicting Racial Identification from Income, Education, and Self-Esteem
(Regression Coefficients)

	Racial Identification			
	Afrocentrism	Common Fate	Autonomy	Build Pride
Predictors				
Family Income	.04	.04	.15*	.07
Education	.67*	.30*	.31*	.54*
Self-Esteem	−.04	.02	.07	−.16
Constant	.27	.45	.23	.14
Multiple R	.325	.140	.240	.156
R-squared	.106	.020	.057	.024
(N)	(503)	(595)	(587)	(559)

Note: *$p < .05$; all of the variables were scaled 0–1.

racial solidarity that is tied to income is the desire for black economic autonomy. There is something that rings right about observing that better-off blacks are distinctively more likely to favor the
specific aspect of black pride that is most closely tied to material
well-being for blacks. The second is this: Self-esteem as well as education is a predictor of support for building black pride and black
self-respect. The self-esteem result, it is true, fails to meet the con-
ventional standards of statistical significance, but only by a hair's
breadth. And what is interesting is that the direction of the relationship is just the other way around from the one our initial analyses suggested: rather than taking pride in being black going along
with a higher level of self-esteem, it goes along with a lower level of
self-regard.

The larger lesson that these findings teach is three fold. First, the
politics of black pride is not in any fundamental sense the politics of
class. We did see evidence of a connection between racial identification and income, but only once, and even then it could not be
described as very strong. Second, the politics of black pride should not
be reduced to the politics of self-therapy. Again we saw evidence of a
connection between racial identification and self-esteem, but that
single relationship was the reverse of expected, and it, too, could
hardly be described as strong. This absence of any consistent connection cuts two ways. It suggests that blacks are not drawn to the diverse

expressions of racial pride and solidarity in order to compensate for feelings of personal unworthiness and a lack of self-esteem. But it also suggests that they do not obtain a stronger sense of self-worth by virtue of committing themselves to the racial pride movement. Both these lessons follow from the fact that the appeal of racial pride is not confined to a specific segment of the larger black community. Rather it runs throughout it, and if not in precisely equal measure in every part, then substantially so. Of the differences in background and circumstance, only the amount of education that our black respondents have had is consistently related to the level of their support for racial identification. The consistency of this result, and this is the third aspect of the lesson of our findings, suggests that if we are to understand the appeal of black pride, it is necessary to understand the ideas, the cast of mind, that goes along with it. That is a matter that we can only begin to explore in this study. The light that we can throw is limited. It nonetheless is revealing, as we shall see next.

Conspiratorial Thinking

That much of contemporary black thought is first-rate should not need saying. But it does need saying because merely summarizing some ideas that have won public standing in some black intellectual circles, and been prominently advertised in some black media, risks accusations of sensationalism and of bad faith. A part of the public black rhetoric—an extreme part, to be sure, but not a negligible one either—fuses radical oversimplification and exaggeration in the service of racially charged allegories. These allegories center on the clash between good and bad, defined in racial terms, and are distinguished by the crudity of the terms in which they are drawn. Leonard Jeffries' grotesquely simpleminded distinction between "Sun People" (i.e., blacks), who represent virtue, authenticity, and creativity, and the "Ice People" (i.e., whites), who embody just the opposite, is perhaps the most notorious example.[47] Bound up in these allegorical jeremiads, but reaching well beyond them, is a cast of mind that has helped define the tone of black public rhetoric: conspiratorial thinking.

[47] For some specifics see Howe 1998, p. 270.

The public rhetoric of black activists, however, is one thing. They have their own incentives to make provocative charges, not the least being winning public attention. And just so far as each competes with the others for public attention, there is a general pressure on black leaders and activists to escalate inflammatory rhetoric. But it does not follow, because black activists make sensational charges, that ordinary blacks believe them. To determine whether they do or not, it is necessary to inquire directly what they think: it is not good enough to assume that they think what black leaders say they think. So it is important to explore how ready ordinary blacks are to believe that there are secret, organized, ongoing, massive efforts to suppress, kill, or even wipe out blacks in America.

The answer is of interest in its own right. Just so far as black Americans are ready to believe in conspiracies on the largest possible scale, the temper of mind in the larger black community comes more clearly into view. But exploring the prevalence of conspiratorial thinking of black Americans also is of interest because it makes it possible to answer a still more important question. To what extent, if any, does the contemporary appeal of black identity and solidarity depend on the lure of conspiratorial thinking?

Our concern is thus twofold: to establish the prevalence of conspiratorial thinking in the larger black community and to determine whether there is any connection between it and the appeals of black pride and solidarity. In speaking of conspiratorial thinking, we must emphasize, we are *not* asking whether black Americans believe that they still are victimized by discrimination. They do and they are. The question instead is the readiness of black Americans to believe in the presence of forces, operating on a vast scale, rooted in the very center of American society, and proceeding with the explicit authorization of the government itself, that are bent on the destruction of black America.

As one way of getting a reading on the prevalence of this species of conspiratorial thinking, we asked our respondents if they agree or disagree that:

> The FBI and the CIA make sure that there is a steady supply of guns and drugs in the inner city.

The sweep of this claim is considerable, to say the least. It is not a matter of believing that there are powerful forces, even extraordinarily powerful forces, capable of overriding the legitimate institutions of American society. The claim here goes much further. Violence and crime in the inner cities, on this conspiratorial reasoning, do not point to a breakdown of law and order. On the contrary, inner-city crime and violence are themselves the handiwork of the official forces of law and order. It is the police agencies that are peddling the drugs to blacks in order to chain them to a life of crime, the police agencies that are flooding the ghettoes with guns in order to insure that those crimes will be as violent as possible. In charging that the CIA and the FBI are peddling drugs and distributing guns in the inner city, the claim is not that black-on-black violence is being aggravated by maverick individuals or groups or a broader societal indifference. The charge instead is that it is being directed by forces at the very center of American society, operating with the tacit blessing, and sometimes even the active assistance, of the most powerful political and business institutions, including the very government of America itself.

Yet there is no shortage of blacks willing to declare that this claim of a gigantic government conspiracy against blacks is true. As the top bar of figure 2.8, shows, almost one half of the blacks that we interviewed, 46 percent to be exact, agreed that the principal police agencies of the federal government were themselves responsible for crime and chaos in black communities, and of those who agreed that there was a criminal plot against blacks by the government itself, more than one half did so strongly.

It is possible, in weighing this result, to argue over whether the glass is half-empty or half-full. It is true that about one half of our sample of blacks are ready to claim that the FBI and the CIA are deliberately promoting crime and violence in the inner cities. But of course it also is true that (slightly) more than a half of them reject this charge. As a second line of defense, one could reply that, bizarre as the accusation of FBI and CIA drug– and gun-running is, respectable news sources have publicized it and prominent black politicians have endorsed it. If ordinary blacks are saying it now, it is only because they are repeating what other presumably credible sources already have said. And as a third line of defense, one might argue that, even if this particular allegation is not strictly accurate, judged against the background of what historically has been done to blacks, the main thrust of the charge is not, on its face, incredible.

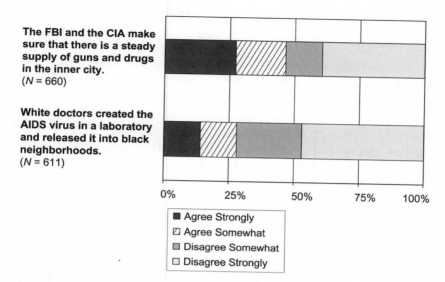

Figure 2.8. Conspiratorial Thinking

We sympathize with the impulse "to contextualize," as the saying goes in academic quarters, this finding of large numbers of blacks being willing to believe in a gigantic *government* conspiracy. No doubt, it is connected to historical experience; no doubt, also, that the particular shape that conspiratorial beliefs take reflects the activity of political and media figures in publicizing and legitimating specific charges and allegations. But however we have gotten to where we are, where we are is that a striking number of black Americans are ready to charge the government itself with directing a conspiracy against them. According to our study, roughly one half of them do so. And that is a fact worth considering. A glass half-filled with a potent liquor can have a considerable impact, and judged by any standard, a readiness to charge that officials responsible for law and order are engaged in what amounts almost to black genocide is a potent idea.

There is, this result suggests, a will to believe extraordinary claims. And it is not a matter of a willingness to believe just one particular allegation. We also asked our respondents whether they agree or disagree that:

White doctors created the AIDS virus in a laboratory and released it into black neighborhoods.

This is a claim of genocide. Whatever one may say about CIA involvement in the ghettoes, there is no reasonable basis whatever for a charge that the AIDS virus was deliberately created by white doctors in order to infect and eliminate blacks. Unlike the charge that fifth-century Greek philosophers copied the ideas of their African predecessors, which is more difficult to gauge because the issues have been obscured by the passage of time, the charge that the AIDS virus was created by white doctors and deliberately set loose in black neighborhoods refers to something that allegedly has just happened, and, in principle, the validity of this charge should therefore be easier to gauge. Baldly put, the claim about AIDS being invented by white doctors and released into black neighborhoods is a paranoid fantasy, unsupported by any evidence. Yet one in every four in our sample agree with it (as the lower bar of figure 2.8 shows).

It is of course reasonable to ask whether this result means what it appears to mean. The people we interviewed all live in Chicago, and although Chicago blacks may be similar to blacks in the country as a whole in many ways, it does not follow that they are similar in every way. And quite apart from whether a susceptibility to believe that AIDS was invented by white doctors is unusually pronounced in Chicago (or metropolitan areas), there is the question of what it actually means to say that AIDS was "created" by white doctors. Perhaps when blacks say that "white doctors created the AIDS virus in a laboratory," they mean only to say that a (new) virus must have been created by somebody, and since medical researchers are disproportionately white, the person who "created" AIDS was most likely white: but this does *not* mean that they invented AIDS in order to harm blacks.[48]

This second line of argument does not strike us as persuasive—after all, in our question we ask "whether white doctors created the AIDS virus . . . and *released it into black neighborhoods."* The assertion that the AIDS virus was released into black neighborhoods, on an ordinary reading, would convey the implication that the disease was

[48] We want to thank Marc Adler, who, on the basis of a focused interview, pointed out the possible ambiguity of intent to us.

let loose with a deliberate intent to harm blacks. Still, it is true that every question is ambiguous to some degree. It is accordingly a fortunate chance that we have another study to draw on to corroborate our own. This second study drew on a national sample representative of the opinions of blacks in the country as a whole, and asked respondents "to tell which choice is most true for you":

> AIDS is a tragic disease with natural origins that is devastating the black community; or, AIDS is a disease that is a result of an antiblack conspiracy.

Several features of this question in the second study deserve to be underscored. For one thing, respondents were presented with alternative formulations that they could choose between, instead of being confined to agreeing or disagreeing with one. For another, the contrast between the two formulations highlights the issue of intent. Is AIDS a disease of natural origins or the product of an antiblack conspiracy? To reject the former and endorse the latter surely eliminates any vapor of ambiguity as to whether the harm was intentional. Notice also that the first alternative puts before the respondent an explanation that is *both* posed in naturalistic terms and *yet* underscores the terrible losses that the black community has suffered. Finally, since the question was asked of a nationally representative sample of blacks, the result addresses the question of whether the results from our sample are exceptional or peculiar. For all of these reasons, the outcome of this second study are all the more striking. Quite simply, the result mirrors our own nearly perfectly. In this second study, 26.1 percent took the position that AIDS was the result of antiblack conspiracy.[49] In ours, 27.7 percent take the position "white doctors created the AIDS virus in a laboratory and released it into black neighborhoods."

The task, however, is not simply to observe that significant numbers of blacks say things like this, but to get some sense of what it means for them to say things like this. On the face of it, charging white doctors with deliberately creating the AIDS virus and the FBI and CIA of running drugs and guns bears the stamp of a paranoid mentality. Without minimizing the elements of suspicion and anger

---

[49] Dawson 2001, table A1.1, pp. 227–33.

that accompany allegations on this order, we believe that it gets things more wrong than right to put the issue in terms of psychological pathology. If it truly were a matter of a paranoid mentality taking hold among black Americans, there should be an across-the-board readiness to charge that conspiracies against blacks are being carried out: and the stronger this across-the-board readiness, the more consistent the responses of blacks should be to the questions on the FBI-CIA and the AIDS virus. There is in fact a statistically significant relationship, and it is positive: blacks who agree with one are more likely to agree with the other. But the size of the relationship is quite moderate.[50]

The fact that if blacks believe in one of these conspiracies they are *not* powerfully more likely to believe in the other is worth underscoring. We have, it is true, only two indicators of a readiness to believe in racial conspiracies. Were we to have more, we might come to a different impression. But on the evidence at hand, the conclusion to draw is that there is *not* a paranoid mentality among black Americans. Some tendency to consistency notwithstanding, there is *not* an elaborate, tightly woven ideology of conspiratorial thinking. These particular conspiracies, in fact, differ in their appeal at some points. For one thing, markedly more of our respondents are ready to believe that the FBI and the CIA are up to no good than are ready to believe that white doctors invented the AIDS virus to eliminate blacks. For another, younger blacks are more likely to believe that the FBI and the CIA are implicated in drugs and guns in the inner cities than are older blacks, while age has no relation to the readiness to believe that the AIDS virus was invented to harm blacks.

All of this is true and important. But there is nonetheless a tendency to consistency on these questions of conspiracy—if you believe one, you are significantly more likely to believe the other. To believe *both* is to be ready to believe pretty much anything about the willingness of white America to harm black America. Accordingly, responses to both conspiracy questions have been combined to form an Index of Conspiratorial Thinking: the higher people's scores on this index, the more of these accusations with which they agree, and the more emphatically they agree with them.

[50] The pearson correlation between the two items is .17.

Conspiratorial Thinking and Black Pride

Are conspiratorial thinking and feeling a sense of racial iden-tification and solidarity connected? Does taking pride in being black sharpen people's sensibilities that they are victims of large, ongoing conspiracies?

It certainly is not obvious that a penchant for conspiratorial thinking should accompany all of the ways in which blacks can express a sense of racial identification. Purely as a logical possibility, black Americans who feel a sense of common fate with other blacks may also be disposed to embrace the notion that white Americans are engaged in massive conspiracies to destroy black America. Psy-chologically, however, this strikes us as strained, to say the least. People surely can feel a sense of affinity with others who are like them in some salient respect without this sense of affinity rendering them susceptible to a paranoid style of political thinking. On the other hand, it is not difficult to see why the suggestion that Greek philosophers in the fifth century purloined their ideas from African predecessors might appeal to a person who believes that govern-ment agencies are engaged in a malevolent conspiracy against black Americans.

The first step is seeing whether, in fact, a penchant for conspira-torial thinking goes hand-in-hand with racial identification. Table 2.5 reports the extent to which different forms of racial identifica-tion are correlated with a susceptibility to engage in conspiratorial thinking.

The results, we should say, surprised us. We had supposed that, with the exception of Afrocentrism, racial identification would have nothing to do with a conspiratorial style of thinking. As you can see in table 2.5, however, they are all related to it to a significant degree. They are not, however, all related to the same degree. Afrocentrism and conspiratorial thinking are, by all the customary standards, tightly tied together. By contrast, the tie between conspiratorial thinking and sharing a sense of common fate with other blacks, or between it and a desire to build black pride, is markedly looser. Finally, a desire to achieve black (economic) autonomy falls approx-imately midway between Afrocentrism, on the one side, and feeling a sense of common fate and desiring to build black pride on the other, in the closeness of its tie to conspiratorial thinking.

TABLE 2.5
Correlations between Conspiratorial Thinking and Racial Identification
(Correlation Coefficients)

	Correlations with Conspiratorial Thinking
Racial Identification	
Autonomy	.35
Afrocentrism	.41
Common Fate	.21
Build Pride	.18

Note: $N = 478$; all $p < .01$.

Given that all of the forms of racial identification are, in a greater or lesser degree, connected to conspiratorial thinking, should we conclude that there is a general, across-the-board connection between a readiness to charge that gigantic conspiracies are being carried out against black Americans and a desire of black Americans to identify themselves as black in America?

Not necessarily. Since each of these forms of racial identification tends to accompany each of the others, there is an obvious risk. A belief in the importance of building black self-respect, for example, may falsely appear to go along with conspiratorial thinking because it is connected to Afrocentrism, which genuinely goes along with conspiratorial thinking.

The problem, technically, is spuriousness. And the most straightforward way to deal with spuriousness is to calculate the relationship between the Index of Conspiratorial Thinking and all of the various forms of racial identification simultaneously, rather than examining each one at a time in isolation. When this is done (see table 2.6), you can see that some forms of racial identification clearly have no intrinsic connection to a paranoid style of political argumentation. This includes a belief that it is important to build black pride and self-respect. It also includes the belief that what happens to other blacks makes a difference to what happens to you—that is, the emergence of a sense of a shared or 'linked' fate. It is important to learn that both of these forms of racial identification have nothing intrinsically to do with a conspiratorial style of thinking. It is easy to slip into thinking in terms of Black Pride in capitalized letters. Think this way and every expression of racial pride and identification

TABLE 2.6
Predicting Conspiratorial Thinking
(Regression Coefficients)

	Coefficients
Predictors	
Autonomy	.18*
Afrocentrism	.33*
Common Fate	.03
Build Pride	.00
Constant	.03
Multiple R	.446
R-squared	.199

Note: $N = 478$; *$p < .05$. All of the variables were scaled 0–1.

becomes like every other: and if any are tied to an inclination to think in overly simplified terms or to demonize others, then all are.

But if some expressions of racial pride have nothing intrinsically to do with a conspiratorial style of thinking, others do. Our results indicate that there is a marked connection between embracing an Afrocentric perspective, on the one hand, and being ready to believe, on the other, that vast, malevolent conspiracies against black Americans are being carried out at this very moment by central institutions of American society and, indeed, by the government itself. You may, to be sure, have expected this given that Afrocentrism has a conspiratorial, accusatory tone to it. But what you may not have expected—certainly we did not—is that the desire for black economic autonomy also is implicated in a conspiratorial style of thinking. The link here, it is true, is not as pronounced as that between Afrocentrism and conspiratorial thinking. Roughly, it is about half the size. But it is there all the same, a reminder, perhaps, of the underside of the desire for control, economic or otherwise.

A Puzzle: Education and Susceptibility to Conspiratorial Thinking

Being well educated or politically informed, as we have seen, increases the chances that blacks will feel a sense of racial identification: that they favor economic autonomy for blacks; that they will feel they share a common fate with other blacks; that they want to build black pride and self-respect; and that they will embrace an Afrocentric perspective. But when it comes to conspiratorial thinking, the reverse should be true. Surely being politically sophisticated, certainly being better educated, should help render blacks less susceptible to an across-the-board willingness to believe in paranoid ideas of racial conspiracies.

The reasons are straightforward. Education strengthens standards of critical judgment. It helps implant skills for evaluating the adequacy of evidence advanced on behalf of claims, as well as the validity of the reasoning behind arguments made in their behalf. As importantly, education helps strengthen the habits of critical judgment. It is not only that the more educated know how to evaluate an argument; they are more likely to do it. And being more likely both to be skilled in critical judgment and to exercise that skill should lead well-educated blacks to be less susceptible to claims of racial conspiracies that invite critical evaluation on their face.

All of this may seem no more than common sense—certainly it seemed so to us. But in fact, it is wrong. How much education blacks have had and how ready they are to engage in conspiratorial thinking are unrelated.[51] And, suggesting this is not an aberrant result, how politically well informed blacks are about politics and how susceptible they are to conspiratorial thinking are also unrelated.[52] It is not obvious what interpretation to place on these results. It is true that well-educated and politically sophisticated blacks are not more likely than the more poorly educated and unsophisticated to adopt a conspiratorial manner of thinking. It is just as true, however, that they are not more likely to reject one. Should we take comfort in the former? Or should we face up to the less sanguine implication of the latter: that if the advantage of education does not make black Americans more susceptible to the oversimplifications of conspiratorial thinking, neither does it safeguard them against its appeal? And there is a deeper puzzle. On the one hand, better-educated blacks are no more likely than those who have been poorly

[51] Regressing the Index of Conspiratorial Thinking on education, $b = -.028$, $p = .772$, $r = -.012$.

[52] Regressing the Index of Conspiratorial Thinking on political information, $b = .010$, $p = .230$, $r = .010$.

educated to endorse a conspiratorial style argumentation. On the other hand, better-educated blacks are significantly more likely to endorse claims that the achievements of ancient African civilizations have not been properly acknowledged.

Why should education be positively related to the index of Afrocentrism, which has a conspiratorial tone, but not related, positively or negatively, to conspiratorial thinking? It is not hard to think of possible answers. Perhaps the crucial factor is how outlandish, how farfetched the accusations are. The general claim that Africa has made significant intellectual and scientific contributions is surely right, even if the specific claims about the impact of African philosophers on Greek philosophers in the fifth century or the contribution of African wise men to modern science are not. And just so far as the general claim of black contributions to European civilization is right, since better-educated blacks should be more likely than less well-educated blacks to be aware of the full range of black accomplishments, they should be more disposed to endorse broadly Afrocentric sentiments. By contrast, a claim that the AIDS virus was invented by white doctors and released in black neighborhoods is suspect on its face. And just so far as it is suspect, it will not be specially credible to better-educated blacks.

Alternatively, one might argue that better-educated blacks are more likely to accept accusatory judgments about events in the distant past—such as the slighting of the contributions to science of African wise men—because these accusations, by virtue of being buried in an obscure past, are more difficult to evaluate critically. By contrast, because the kind of claims comprising our measure of conspiratorial thinking—about the deliberate invention of AIDS and FBI-CIA drug peddling and gun selling—refer to what is happening now, for better-educated blacks they are easier to form a critical judgment about.

Both lines of argument are possible, but to us they do not seem plausible. For one thing, it is very hard to get a fix on what it means to say that one accusation is more suspect than another. In what sense, exactly, is a claim that "African wise men who lived hundreds of years ago do not get enough credit for their contributions to modern science" less implausible than the claim that "the FBI and the CIA make sure that there is a steady supply of guns and drugs in the inner city?" And it is not obviously right to claim that the reason the better educated are not more likely to claim that the AIDS virus was invented by white doctors and released in black neighborhoods is because they have an epistemological advantage in assessing truth claims about the present. After all, it has been suggested that the reason that the AIDS claim is plausible, bizarre as it might seem on first hearing, is because of the history of infamous medical experiments, the Tuskegee scandal among them, inflicted on African Americans.[53] If so, since better-educated blacks are more likely to be knowledgeable about the history of blacks in America, they should be *more* likely than poorly educated blacks to endorse the AIDS conspiracy claim. But they are not: they are as likely, but no more so.

In any case, both of these attempts at explanation evade the nub of the problem. For if it is true that better-educated blacks are not more likely than poorly educated blacks to endorse questionable claims of conspiracy, it also is true that they are not *less* likely than poorly educated blacks to do so. And the obvious question to put, therefore, is: Why are better-educated blacks not *more* likely to practice higher standards of critical thinking and therefore reject claims that, certainly in the case of AIDS, but arguably also in that of official government conspiracies, breach ordinary canons of plausibility?

As we thought through this puzzle, a possible solution occurred to us. It is consensually agreed that education increases people's exposure to the ideas in circulation and their ability to see the relevance of these ideas to their personal concerns. For both of these reasons, it is widely (though not necessarily consensually) agreed that the better educated blacks are, the more likely they will be to endorse contemporary expressions of racial pride and identity, including Afrocentrism.[54] But believing in ideas of racial identity and solidarity is likely to have consequences for how people see the

---

[53] Dawson 2001, p. 121.

[54] Allen et al. 1989, for example, take the position that education is not related to racial solidarity. The difference between their view and the standard one is more appearance than reality. Their actual finding is not that education is not related to racial solidarity, but that it is not directly related. Thus, they find that education leads to greater exposure to black mass media, and exposure to black mass media, in turn, is related to racial solidarity. The point is not that education does not matter, but rather that they suggest (one of) the mechanisms, or reasons, that it does matter.

world around them. The more that issues of black autonomy and of white recognition of past injustices done to blacks are at the center of their thoughts, the more receptive that blacks are likely to be to allegations of current injustices—even if these allegations are put in extreme terms.

If this line of reasoning is right, a possible solution to the puzzle of education's apparent failure to promote close scrutiny of far-fetched claims about racial conspiracies suggests itself. One effect of education is to promote critical thinking, to enable Americans to assess the cogency of claims and the evidence adduced in their behalf, and thus to help them to resist the lure of oversimplified reasoning. And by promoting the habits and skills of critical thinking among Americans, black as well as white, education *decreases* the appeal of conspiratorial thinking. But education also has another effect among blacks. By increasing the likelihood that they will be exposed to the ideas now in circulation in the black community, such as Afrocentrism, education also *increases* the likelihood that black Americans will support contemporary expressions of racial identification that legitimate and strengthen an accusatory and conspiratorial frame of mind.

If this reasoning is right, education has conflicting effects. Its direct effect is to decrease the appeal of conspiratorial thinking by strengthening standards of critical judgment. Its indirect effect, however, is to increase the appeal of conspiratorial thinking by facilitating the adoption of ideas like Afrocentrism, which, in turn, strengthen the appeal of conspiratorial thinking. Since education's direct and indirect effects are opposite in direction, each will tend to cancel out the other. The result: an impression that, all in all, education neither weakens nor strengthens conspiratorial thinking. Which is just what we have observed.

In the imagery of causal modeling, we have a three-variable problem: conspiratorial thinking, which is the dependent variable (that is, the one we wish to explain); education, which is the independent variable (that is, the one we believe in part explains conspiratorial thinking); and Afrocentrism, which is a mediating variable (that is, one that in part explains the effect of education on conspiratorial thinking). Graphically, the solid arrow in figure 2.9, running directly from education to conspiratorial thinking, represents the direct effect of education; while the dotted arrow, running first from edu-

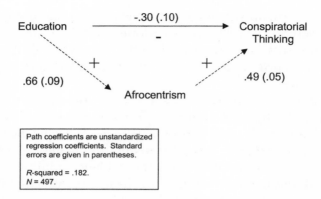

Figure 2.9. Path Diagram Showing Conspiratorial Thinking Predicted by Education and Afrocentrism

cation to Afrocentrism and then from Afrocentrism to conspiratorial thinking, represents education's indirect effect. The strength of each path in the model is summarized by the coefficient beside each arrow.[55] Look first at the direct path. Education clearly has a significant *negative* direct effect on conspiratorial thinking: the better educated blacks are, the less likely they are to embrace a conspiratorial style of thinking. Now look at the indirect paths. Education just as clearly has a significant *positive* effect on conspiratorial thinking: the better educated blacks are, the more likely they are to embrace Afrocentrism: and the more likely they are to embrace Afrocentrism, the more likely they are to embrace a conspiratorial style of thinking. And when you do the arithmetic of calculating education's total effect, the result is that education's direct and indirect effects approximately cancel out.[56]

In short, education, considered by itself, does combat a susceptibility to simplistic, conspiratorial thinking among black Americans. But by promoting ideas like Afrocentrism, education also strengthens the susceptibility of black Americans to conspiratorial thinking.

---

[55] As always, we report the unstandardized regression coefficients with all variables scored from 0 to 1. The numbers in parentheses are their standard errors.

[56] Since education's indirect effect has two links, it is the product of education's impact on Afrocentrism *and* Afrocentrism's effect on conspiratorial thinking.

Reprise

Black Americans' sense of identity as blacks in America finds expression in a number of forms, among them a desire that blacks exercise a greater measure of control over the lives of blacks; a feeling that, because you are black, what affects other blacks affects you; a desire to build black pride and self-respect; and an insistence that the historic accomplishments of blacks be acknowledged.

Some of these ideas—for example, a feeling that one shares a common fate with other blacks—are so widespread in the larger black community as to be nearly consensual. Others—for example, the view that blacks should control the economy in black neighborhoods or that blacks have a duty to shop at black-owned businesses—are more contested. These ideas of racial identification nonetheless are not separate, unconnected. They have a common core. Black Americans who believe in one tend to believe in the others. All are, at bottom, ways of underscoring both the distinctiveness that blacks feel by virtue of being black and the pride they take in this sense of distinctiveness. They embody, in a word, the politics of identity.

Our results suggest that two of the most familiar stories about the politics of identity miss the mark. The first has to do with the psychology of identity politics. A common argument for, and explanation of, the racial pride movement is that it gives blacks just that— a sense of pride.[57] To our knowledge, no study has directly shown this to be so, and the results of our study suggest that it is not so. Purely as a matter of fact, there does not, once the effects of education are taken into account, appear to be any systematic or substantial connection between the readiness of blacks to express any of the forms of racial identification that we have surveyed and their level of self-esteem. The second story has to do with the sociology of identity politics. On this view, black pride, in at least some of its manifestations, is essentially a middle-class movement. We have found some connection between how strongly blacks identify themselves as black with how well-off they are. With the exception only of support for black economic autonomy, however, this connection

[57] Rhea 1997.

appears to be a function of the fact that blacks who are well-off tend also to be well-educated.

The common thread that we have found running through all of these different forms of racial identification—of feeling a sense of linked fate with other blacks, of wanting economic autonomy for blacks, of wishing to build black pride, of insisting on the historic achievements of blacks—is that all are embraced more often, and more strongly, the better educated and the more politically informed blacks are. Ideas of racial pride are, in this sense, the ideas of the brightest black Americans. But some of these expressions of racial pride are notable because they are conspicuously crude and oversimplified—we have in mind here the claims made under the banner of Afrocentrism. How is it that the best and brightest accept ideas that are very far from the brightest and the best of ideas? This is a paradox that we will return to in considering the temper of contemporary racial politics.

What we wish to do now is take up a pair of questions of fundamental interest. First, does valuing being black lead blacks to devalue those who are not black, including Asians, Latinos, and Jews? Second, to what extent does a climate of opinion in which charges of racial conspiracies are legitimate contribute to black anti-Semitism?

3 Conflict

In its early years, the civil rights movement pledged itself to cooperation: cooperation between blacks and whites, between blacks and Jews. After the movement stalled in the mid1960s, conflict eclipsed cooperation: conflict between blacks and Jews, blacks and Koreans, blacks and whites.

Every conflict has its unique aspects—its own history, its individual context. But there also are points of similarity, and three types of explanatory stories have generally been told when blacks clash with other minorities. The first of these explanations emphasizes competition for public benefits. On this view, blacks clash with other minorities because they are competing for jobs, for priority in advancement, and for political influence more broadly. The first explanation thus focuses outwards—on a struggle for scarce resources—and is motivated by a desire to be better-off. The second explanation focuses inwards—on the welter of resentments, insecurities, and anger that can well up within individuals. On this view, the irrational hostility at the core of prejudice accounts for the rage marking conflicts between blacks and Jews or between blacks and Asians. Finally, the third explanation points to the inherent divisiveness of identity politics. On this third view, conflict between blacks and other minorities is fanned by black pride.

The truth or falsity of each of the three explanations is independent of the truth or falsity of either of the others. We shall accordingly examine all three. In the process, we shall try to answer a number of questions that are, without exaggeration, controversial. For example, to what extent are African Americans ready to support affirmative action if, instead of their reaping the benefits, they flow to another group, say, Mexican Americans? Or to give another example: Are the views of blacks and whites about Jews essentially alike or are African Americans distinctively anti-Semitic? And whatever the attitudes of black Americans toward Jews in the abstract, do considerations of black pride and solidarity widen the gulf between them when they come into conflict? Or, to offer a final example: What lies behind the readiness of some blacks to charge others with being racists? Does it arise out of a sense of solidarity and identification with other blacks, or is it spurred by some other, quite different factor?

We believe that you will find some, and perhaps all, of the answers to these questions genuinely surprising.

Fighting over Political Spoils: Affirmative Action

Affirmative action programs were originally set up for black Americans; indeed, would not have been set up *but* for black Americans. But blacks, even if they are the best-advertised beneficiaries, now are only one of many minorities benefiting from these programs. That means that a whole range of benefits—from special set-asides in government contracts, to special admission slots for universities and professional schools, to special provisions for political representation—increasingly have to be split. And, usually, more for "them" means less for "us."

It could be argued that women, not blacks, have always been the principal beneficiaries of affirmative action. But the rewards of cooperation obscured the rigors of competition between blacks and white women; at any rate they did so in the beginning. By contrast, the waves of immigration over the last three decades have redefined the political arithmetic of affirmative action. Latinos already outnumber blacks in many cities and in some states. Hispanic Americans inevitably are claiming the benefits of their numbers under regimes of minority representation and affirmative action. And given the rules of the political game, they will be getting more and more. Hence, according to the first explanatory story, the hostility of African Americans to Hispanic Americans.

One can point to evidence lending credibility to this story of group competition. Lawrence Bobo and Vincent Hutchings have shown that a substantial number of black Americans complain that more jobs for Mexican Americans means fewer jobs for black Americans;[58] better housing for Mexican Americans, less housing for black Americans; more opportunities for advancement for Mexican Americans, less opportunities for black Americans; and vice versa.[59] This is evidence, according to Bobo and Hutchings, that African Americans square off against Mexican Americans because each calculates that they will be worse off if the other is better off.

This is a plausible conjecture. The problem is that it takes for granted just what it is supposed to explain—namely, that African Americans will support a policy if fellow blacks are its beneficiaries but not if Hispanic Americans are. Is this true?

In our first study on the politics of race, *The Scar of Race*, we designed an experiment, the "Equal Opportunity" experiment, to assess racial discrimination. The idea was that half of the time white Americans would be asked whether the government should assure equal opportunity for women to succeed; the other half of the time, they would be asked whether it should assure equal opportunity for blacks to succeed. The results showed that a substantial number of whites continue to discriminate against blacks; that is, whites were more likely to believe that government should assure equal opportunity if women rather than blacks benefit.

This result spoke to the reality of white racism on which our first study focused. But our eyes also were caught by another result. In the course of analyzing the "Equal Opportunity" experiment, we realized that we could turn it inside out. In addition to asking whether whites practice a double standard against blacks, we could also ask whether blacks practice a double standard in favor of fellow blacks. If it is true that whites are more likely to believe that the government should promote equal opportunity for women than for blacks, is it also true that blacks are more likely to believe that it should promote equal opportunity for blacks than for whites and other nonblacks?

The Survey Research Center at the University of California at Berkeley carried out our first study as well as this, our latest. We went around the Center, informally asking colleagues to bet on the outcome of the Equal Opportunity Experiment. Are blacks more sup-

[58] Bobo and Hutchings 1996.

[59] A roughly equal number of Mexican Americans, they also show, believe the same about black Americans.

portive of government assuring equal opportunity for their fellow blacks than for women? Everyone at the Center, black and white alike, made the same prediction. Blacks would be more sympathetic to the needs of fellow blacks and therefore more likely to back the idea that the government should secure equal opportunity for fellow blacks than for women. But on testing it, the universally shared prediction of black double standards proved wrong. Our black respondents played no favorites. They were just as likely to back the claims of women to government assistance as those of blacks.

This result was based on a limited sample of blacks, but we found it riveting nonetheless. It suggested to us that ordinary black Americans make their decision, not in terms of a calculus of political spoils, but on the basis of political principles. If they believed in activist government for blacks, they were just as likely to believe in it for those who were not black.

We are not implying, and it would be a mistake to infer, that this finding means that blacks do not care whether a policy benefits blacks. We are saying that it led us to take seriously the possibility that blacks might treat the claims of blacks and of Latinos, notwithstanding the strains between them, evenhandedly. We have then two possibilities. If, as Bobo and Hutchings suggest, blacks play favorites because there is a competition for benefits, then they should support a policy or not depending on whether it benefits blacks or not. If, as we suggest, blacks are evenhanded, blacks should be as likely to support a program when it benefits Mexican Americans as when it benefits African Americans.

To see which is true, favoritism or evenhandedness, we carried out a "Switching the Beneficiary" experiment. The experiment focuses on the policy area where the stakes for group competition are highest, affirmative action. In one experimental condition, we asked one half of the respondents whether they favored or opposed "large companies having quotas to make sure a certain number of blacks are hired;" in the other, we asked the other half exactly the same question except about hiring Mexican Americans. Crucially, each half has no way to tell that the other half is being asked about whether a different group should benefit.

Are blacks willing to tip the scales in favor of fellow blacks? The answer has two parts. On the one hand, judged in terms of the level of support for affirmative action, our black respondents are strik-

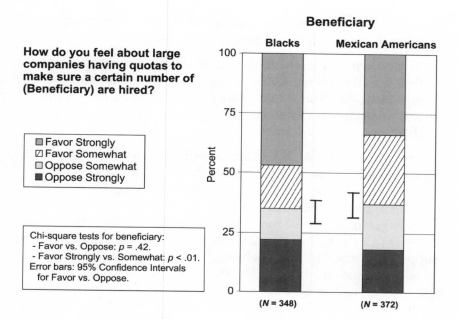

Beneficiary

How do you feel about large companies having quotas to make sure a certain number of (Beneficiary) are hired?

- ▨ Favor Strongly
- ▨ Favor Somewhat
- ▢ Oppose Somewhat
- ▪ Oppose Strongly

Chi-square tests for beneficiary:
- Favor vs. Oppose: *p* = .42.
- Favor Strongly vs. Somewhat: *p* < .01.
Error bars: 95% Confidence Intervals for Favor vs. Oppose.

(N = 348)   (N = 372)

Figure 3.1. Support for Racial Quotas

ingly evenhanded: 65 percent of respondents support job quotas for blacks; 63 percent for Mexican Americans—statistically the two numbers are indistinguishable. On the other hand, judged in terms of *intensity* of support, our black respondents express stronger support for quotas if blacks are to benefit from them than if Mexican Americans are (see figure 3.1). Shall we say that African Americans are evenhanded in treating the claims of African and Mexican Americans? Or should we conclude that they favor their fellow blacks?

This issue of favoritism or evenhandedness goes to the character of minority politics. We therefore planned in advance a pair of experiments to guard against the danger of being misled by the results of just one. The strategy was the same for both. Ask one half of our sample whether a form of affirmative action is a good idea for African Americans; ask the other half whether exactly the same thing is a good idea for Mexican Americans. There was one difference, however. The form of affirmative action in the first Switching the Beneficiary experiment, job quotas, was familiar to nearly everyone. The form in the second experiment, racial redistricting, is not familiar to many. For this experiment, we asked:

In areas where a large number of [blacks/Mexican Americans] live, how do you feel about changing the boundaries for congressional districts so that more [blacks/Mexican Americans] will be elected to Congress? Are you in favor of or opposed to this?

The results of the Redistricting Experiment (shown in figure 3.2) generally match those of the first of the Switching the Beneficiary experiments. On the one side, strong majorities support racial redistricting to benefit both blacks and Mexican Americans. The majority is larger in the case of the former (83 percent) than in that of the latter (71 percent). But the obvious point is that black Americans support redistricting overwhelmingly whether black Americans or Mexican Americans benefit. On the other side, if you look at the intensity of support, you will see that blacks are much more likely to *strongly* favor redistricting when blacks are to benefit (64 percent) than when Mexican Americans are to benefit (27 percent).

The results of both experiments are thus mutually supportive. In both, a politically dominating majority of black Americans favor assistance for both blacks and Mexican Americans. Also in both, blacks more strongly favor assistance for blacks than for Mexican Americans. What is the right conclusion to draw from this pair of findings: that blacks tend to play favorites, or that they tend to be evenhanded?

One argument is that being evenhanded means reacting identically to those with whom one has no bond and to those with whom one does have a common bond. A different argument is that evenhandedness requires being as ready to lend a helping hand to members of another group as to members of your own, even if you extend your hand more enthusiastically to members of your own group. We recognize that reasonable people can differ as to which is the right standard for evenhandedness. We also recognize the risk of special pleading. Given the injustices done to blacks, the temptation sometimes is to search for a justification of what one otherwise would not seek to justify. But a standard of judgment should fit what is being judged. It asks too much of people, whatever group they belong to, that they must not only treat people the same whether

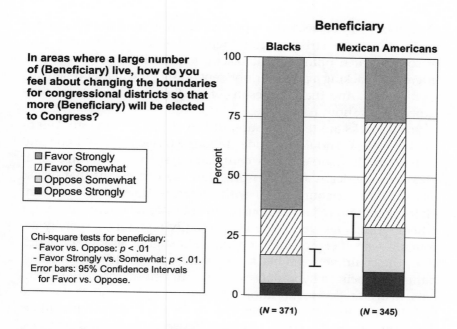

In areas where a large number of (Beneficiary) live, how do you feel about changing the boundaries for congressional districts so that more (Beneficiary) will be elected to Congress?

■ Favor Strongly
☑ Favor Somewhat
□ Oppose Somewhat
■ Oppose Strongly

Chi-square tests for beneficiary:
- Favor vs. Oppose: $p < .01$
- Favor Strongly vs. Somewhat: $p < .01$.
Error bars: 95% Confidence Intervals for Favor vs. Oppose.

Figure 3.2. Support for Racial Redistricting

they belong to their group or not, but must also feel the same toward them whether they share a common bond or not. Blacks may have a special measure of sympathy for fellow blacks, just as Jews may have a special measure of sympathy for fellow Jews, without either group necessarily treating the other unfairly. Moreover, in the case immediately before us, it surely is possible to advance an argument on the merits that the historical experience and objective conditions of blacks in America warrant a measure of assistance that those of Latinos in America may not. However that may be, in politics what matters decisively is what side of the fence you come down on when it comes to affirmative action, in support or in opposition.

If this is a reasonable definition of evenhandedness, then the results of both Switching the Beneficiary experiments demonstrate the readiness of African Americans to back affirmative action whether it benefits African Americans or Mexican Americans. If, however, you require that blacks must react identically to the claims of nonblacks and blacks, the results of the Switching the Beneficiary experiments are striking nonetheless. For it has become part of sophisticated opinion that blacks' approach to politics is self-interested, backing a policy or not depending on whether it benefits them or not. And that, the results of the Switching the Beneficiary Experiments show, is not true.

But if blacks are ready to support the claims of Mexican Americans, then how should we understand the observation of Bobo and Hutchings that some blacks complain that they are worse-off if Mexican Americans are better-off. They say this means that blacks feel they are in competition with Mexican Americans. But complaining that more jobs or housing or educational opportunities for "them" means less for "us" may primarily represent a socially acceptable way of expressing deep-seated hostilities and resentments. If so, the strain between black Americans and Mexican Americans, rather than being a byproduct of a real competition for material benefits, instead reflects an irrational animosity and prejudice that one feels for the other. We therefore turn to the issue of black prejudice. Since the bitterest conflict has been between blacks and Jews, we focus on the question of black anti-Semitism.

Are Black Americans More Anti-Semitic Than White Americans?

We focus on one particular form of prejudice: anti-Semitism. The strains between African Americans and Jewish Americans have been a source of distress and regret. They have also engendered a long and divisive debate over responsibility for the conflict between the two.[60] To many Jews, it seems evident that anti-Semitism is especially pronounced among blacks. To many blacks, including blacks who detest anti-Semitism, it seems equally evident that the charge of black anti-Semitism represents moral blackmail.[61] What does it mean, as Adolph Reed asks, to speak of black anti-Semitism? Certainly some blacks dislike Jews, but so do some nonblacks. Why not just speak of anti-Semitism? Why focus on a few notorious figures—

[60] See, for example, Berman 1994; Kaufman 1988; Dinnerstein 1994; Franklin, Grant, Kletnick, and McNeil 1998; Lerner and West 1995; and Rieder 1985.

[61] For a strongly argued and thoughtful discussion, see Reed 1999.

Khalid Muhammed, former spokesman for Louis Farrakhan and the Black Muslims, for example—who are marginal to the larger black community: indeed, who are well known partly because they are marginal. The very suggestion that they are representative, argues Reed, is a form of stereotyping, an example of perceiving all blacks to be essentially alike. And isn't the charge of black anti-Semitism a blatant example of a double standard? Does it not rest, at bottom, on an insistence that blacks, to be treated as equal to whites, must be free of prejudice in a way that whites never have been and never will be?

Some of these questions are valid. But it does not follow that examining the question of anti-Semitism among blacks is invalid. What is at issue is a matter of fact. Are levels of anti-Semitism roughly the same among white and black Americans or are they significantly different?

The results of earlier studies, even in the face of markedly different sample designs and measurement approaches, are broadly consistent, though not entirely so. Gary Marx's pioneering study in the mid-1960s, though finding blacks more likely than whites to endorse negative stereotypes of Jews, found them to be so to any substantial degree only with respect to negative economic stereotypes.[62] Subsequent studies have pointed to a more consistent pattern of differences, with blacks being systematically more likely to endorse negative stereotypes of Jews.[63] For our study, we selected a number of questions to assess anti-Semitism that had been developed, tested, and validated by the Survey Research Center at the University of California at Berkeley in a multifaceted study of anti-Semitism in the United States, exploring religious, economic, social, and historical sources of prejudice against Jews.[64] A whole battery of questions about attitudes toward Jews was developed, exploring American ideas about longstanding stereotypes of Jews, discrimination in hiring, residential discrimination, intermarriage, social discrimination, and political involvement of Jews, among other things. From this pool of standard questions, we selected five. They are:

[62] See Marx 1967, pp. 126–67.

[63] See Sigelman, Shockey, and Sigelman 1993 and Martire and Clark 1982, table 4.5, p. 42.

[64] Charles Y. Glock was the founding director of the Survey Research Center and the principal investigator of the prejudice research program.

Most Jews are ambitious and work hard to succeed.

Most Jews are more willing than other people to use shady practices to get ahead in life.

Most Jews believe that they are better than other people.

Most Jews are inclined to be more loyal to Israel than to America.

Most Jews don't care what happens to people who aren't Jewish.

Respondents were asked whether they agree strongly, agree somewhat, disagree somewhat, or disagree strongly with each.

You will notice that the first question, asking whether "most Jews are ambitious and work hard to succeed" is positive in tone. We began with this item following our standard practice, not because we planned to make use of it, but to give respondents an opportunity to say something positive about Jews in order that they should then be free to say something negative, if they truly wished to say something negative.[65] The next four questions cover a litany of standard allegations: of unscrupulousness in business, of excess pride, of tribal loyalties and concerns. The wording is either identical, or highly similar, to measures of anti-Semitism in other studies.

What does the evidence suggest about the comparative levels of anti-Semitism among black Americans and among white Americans? By drawing on a survey of a national cross section of the American public that we carried out in 1991, The National Race and Politics Survey, we can compare the attitudes of whites and blacks toward Jews.[66] In both studies, the wording of the questions was

[65] In all of our previous studies using these items, we had noticed that positively worded items are only poorly intercorrelated with negative ones; that is, that even people who are strongly prejudiced against Jews are prepared to acknowledge that they can have some positive qualities. This study was no exception. The (average) correlation of the one positive item with the other four negative ones is .08.

[66] For a description of this survey, see Sniderman and Carmines 1997. The study was funded by the National Science Foundation and was carried out in 1991 on a nationwide random-digit telephone sample by the University of California, Berkeley, Survey Research Center. The target population for the study was all English-speaking adults, 18 years of age or older, residing in households with telephones, within the 48 contiguous states. There were 2,223 interviews completed, with a 65.3 percent response rate.

exactly the same. So, too, was the method of asking them—over the telephone. And, so, too, was the order in which they were asked.

How far, if at all, is there a problem of black anti-Semitism? Note first the remarkable readiness of both blacks and whites to attribute a positive characteristic to Jews. Nearly everyone agrees that Jews are ambitious and want to work hard: 82 percent of blacks in our Chicago study, and 95 percent of whites nationally agree with this positive characterization of Jews: and what is more, the proportion who agree strongly with this positive characterization of Jews is very close for both samples (see figure 3.3).

What, then, about the readiness of blacks to find fault with Jews? Are they more likely, less likely, or perhaps neither more nor less likely, than whites to endorse negative stereotypes of Jews?

Quite simply, our black respondents are more likely to endorse negative stereotypes of Jews, usually markedly so, and more likely, moreover, to do so strongly. Consider the issue of honesty. Almost one out of every two blacks in our Chicago sample agree that "most Jews are more willing than other people to use shady practices to get ahead in life," compared to one out of three whites in the national sample. What's more, blacks are twice as likely as whites to agree strongly that Jews use "shady practices." The differences between whites and Chicago blacks are not always this large. One's eye inevitably is caught by striking differences. So it is important to underline that sometimes the key point is the similarity, not the dissimilarity, of white and black views of Jews. Thus, roughly the same proportion of both, about one-third, say that most Jews believe that "they are better than other people," though again our Chicago blacks are approximately twice as likely as whites to agree strongly with this negative characterization of Jews. Looking at the results from a different angle, what stands out is the number and variety of points on which Jews are vulnerable to criticism whether from whites or blacks. Substantial numbers of both black and white Americans charge Jews with being clannish, agreeing that "most Jews don't care what happens to people who aren't Jewish." And an even sorer point is the issue of divided loyalties, with even larger numbers of both white and black Americans agreeing that "most Jews are inclined to be more loyal to Israel than to America."

Nevertheless, what is striking is the consistency of the differences between blacks and whites. According to the data, blacks are always

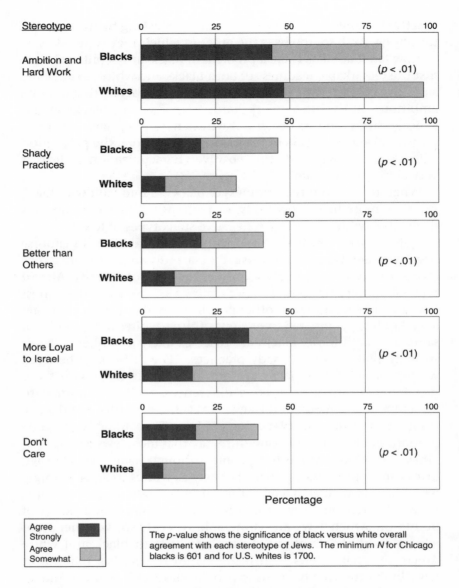

Figure 3.3. Comparing Black and White Agreement with Stereotypes of Jews

more likely than whites to express a negative view of Jews, whatever the specific point of criticism. This consistency matters. It means that blacks do not score higher on measures of anti-Semitism merely because they are readier to accept a narrow, restricted set of negative stereotypes of Jews—for example, being untrustworthy in business—that arguably might be tied to historical economic relations between Jews and blacks in inner cities.

But does it follow that blacks in the United States as a whole are more anti-Semitic than whites? It certainly does not follow that what is true of blacks in Chicago is true of blacks everywhere. And when it comes to the issue of anti-Semitism there is a stare-in-your-face reason why blacks in Chicago may differ from blacks elsewhere. Chicago is the center for Black Muslims, and under the leadership of Louis Farrakhan, anti-Semitism has been a banner theme. Farrakhan and the Black Muslims are active and visible nationally. But it seems a reasonable bet that they are more active and better known in Chicago than in many other places. Black anti-Semitism may get a boost there that it does not elsewhere.

It is therefore necessary to consider to what extent the views of blacks in Chicago toward Jews are similar to, or different from, those of blacks in the country as a whole. To get a comparative view, we again take advantage of the national survey of Americans, now comparing the reactions of blacks from Chicago and blacks from the country as a whole to negative stereotypes of Jews.[67] This comparison, we want to emphasize, is a crude one. Because black Americans make up a comparatively small share of the country as a whole (roughly on the order of 12 percent), they make up a correspondingly small portion of any random sample of Americans as a whole. Since the precision of a sample is tied to the size of the sample, the contrast between the attitudes of blacks from the Chicago sample and blacks from the national sample is crude in the specific sense that we can tell whether the two groups of blacks differ in the population only if they differ by a great deal in the two samples.

If you compare the levels of anti-Semitism in the Chicago sample of blacks and the national sample of blacks, you will see the similarity of their attitudes toward Jews (figure 3.4). Within the limits of precision available to us, both are equally likely to agree that most Jews

[67] See the description of the national sample in the previous note.

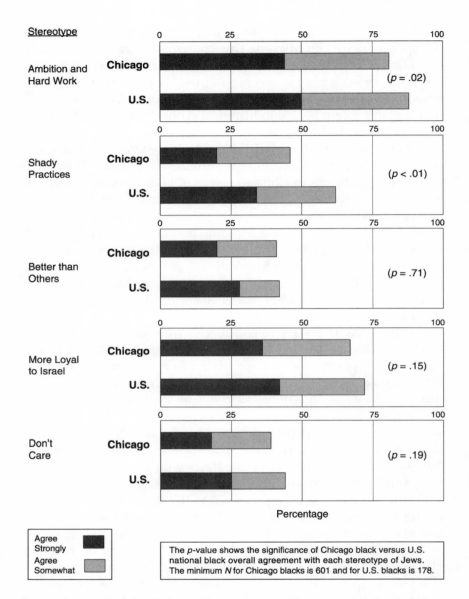

Figure 3.4. Comparing Black Agreement with Stereotypes of Jews: Chicago Sample versus National Sample

"believe that they are better than other people;" that they "don't care what happens to people who aren't Jewish;" and that they "are inclined to be more loyal to Israel than to America." To be sure, blacks nationally appear to be slightly more likely than blacks from Chicago to endorse the idea that "most Jews are more willing than other people to use shady practices to get ahead in life." Obviously, it would be a mistake to make too much of this one difference.

The evidence from our surveys thus points to the conclusion that the level of anti-Semitism is significantly higher among black Americans than among white Americans. The only other source of systematic evidence of which we are aware are the surveys commissioned by the Anti-Defamation League.[68] We therefore have arranged a comparison between our results and theirs, using their two most recent national surveys, one conducted in 1992 and one in 1998. Their measure of anti-Semitism, though similar in content, uses the older true-false answer format. It is not possible, therefore, to compare responses to individual questions about Jews in their study and ours.[69]

It is possible to compare responses to overall measures of anti-Semitism, however. Both possible and desirable. It nearly always is better to have a measure with multiple components rather than to rely on a single indicator, and for the measurement of prejudice having multiple indicators is mandatory. Any given individual can interpret any given question in an idiosyncratic way because of his or her personal experiences. Endorsing this or that negative stereotype about a group accordingly is not necessarily a proof of prejudice. Better evidence is consistently, systematically, endorsing negative stereotypes. Put straightforwardly, the more consistently a person attributes negative characteristics to a group, the more prejudiced he or she is.[70] The quartet of questions in our study about negative stereotypes of Jews is well suited for the task at hand. Responses to them are highly correlated. A person who endorses one negative stereotype, whatever it is, is very much more likely than one who rejects it to endorse every other negative stereotype.[71]

---

[68] We obtained the data presented here from the Anti-Defamation League.

[69] We only have the summated data to work with anyway.

[70] For a systematic discussion of alternative theoretical and operational definitions of prejudice, see chapter 2 of Sniderman et al. 2000.

[71] The mean inter-item correlation is .42.

TABLE 3.1
Ratio of Black to White Anti-Semitism
(Ratios from Three National Surveys)

	Survey		
	National Race and Politics: 1991	ADL Survey: 1992	ADL Survey: 1998
Anti-Semitism Score			
High	1.7	2.2	3.8
Middle	1.0	1.2	1.4
Low	.5	.3	.4

Source: 1991 Race and Politics Survey and Anti-Defamation League surveys from 1992 and 1998.

Accordingly, when answers to the four questions are summed together, constituting the overall measure of anti-Semitism, the measure has a quite satisfactory degree of reliability.[72]

It is possible now to compare responses to their overall measure of anti-Semitism and ours. Both their measure and ours have been divided into three categories: high, middle, and low. Just so far as blacks are more anti-Semitic than whites, blacks will be more likely to score in the "high" category. Conversely, just so far as whites are less anti-Semitic than blacks, they will be disproportionately likely to score in the "low" category. For each study—their two national studies, and the previously mentioned National Race and Politics Survey—we have calculated the ratio of black to white proportions in each of the three categories of the anti-Semitism measure. As you can see in table 3.1, in each of the three studies blacks are disproportionately *more* likely to score in the "high" category: indeed, averaging across the three studies, blacks are about twice as likely to do so. Conversely, blacks are disproportionately less likely to score in the "low" category: again averaging over the three studies, less than half as likely to do so. If there is any difference between our results and the ADL results, it is that their surveys show blacks to be more anti-Semitic compared to whites than do ours.

[72] For the Chicago sample, alpha = .75; for the national white sample, alpha = .77; for the portion of the national sample that is black, alpha = .69.

Race and Anti-Semitism

Observing that levels of anti-Semitism are significantly higher among blacks than among whites is deeply ambiguous. It is ambiguous because black and white Americans clearly differ in ways that may be correlated with a susceptibility to anti-Semitism. For example, on average blacks are less educated than whites and in general the less educated are more susceptible to anti-Semitism.[73] But just so far as this is true, there is an obvious risk of misinterpretation. Blacks may have higher levels of anti-Semitism, not because being black and being anti-Semitic are connected, but instead because being black is connected to having less educational opportunity. It is necessary, therefore, to consider not only the levels, but also the sources, of anti-Semitism.

A number of basic socio-psychological factors that lie behind anti-Semitism are well established.[74] The amount of formal schooling just picks one element of a larger complex. The more cosmopolitan are people's outlooks, the more attentively they follow current events; and the better stocked their fund of information about public affairs, the less susceptible they are to anti-Semitism. Nor is it hard to understand why all this is so. Prejudice is now at odds with the norms of the official culture, and whatever increases the chances of people being aware of the norms of the official culture, as education and cognitive sophistication manifestly do, decreases the chances of their acquiring views at odds with it.[75] An individual's basic psychological makeup is yet another factor, and it is of approximately the same order of importance as formal education in affecting individuals' susceptibility to prejudice. To abbreviate crudely, the more hostile, cynical, and suspicious people tend to be, the more susceptible they are to prejudice.[76] And of course, a whole variety of other factors can matter. Age is one. Being older increases the chances of being prejudiced, if only because when those who are older now were being socialized as children, the norms were markedly less tolerant than they are now. Gender also can make a difference, in this instance

[73] Selznick and Steinberg 1969.
[74] For an older, but still excellent, review, see Quinley and Glock 1977.
[75] The classic locus of this argument is Selznick and Steinberg 1969.
[76] Duckitt 1992.

confirming stereotypes, with women being less, and men more, susceptible to intolerance. Other factors that can matter would include
social class; the region of the country where people live or grew
up—think of the persisting differences between the South and the
rest of the country;[77] religion—consider the potential impact particularly of certain fundamentalist doctrines that stress the necessity of
accepting Christ as a personal savior.[78]

Many of these factors, alone or in combination, may account for
all, or some part, of the difference we have observed between black
and white levels of anti-Semitism. Blacks, after all, are less likely to
be well off or to have had the full run of educational opportunities,
and therefore less likely to enjoy the advantages that flow from
both. Then, too, they are more likely to live in, or at any rate to have
been born, in the South, and therefore are more likely to be bur-
dened by the disadvantages that follow from growing up in a region
of the country that is relatively less tolerant. For that matter, blacks
are more likely to belong to Protestant denominations that espouse
fundamentalist tenets, and therefore are more likely to be exposed
to certain beliefs that encourage anti-Semitism.[79]

For any or all of these reasons, the observation that levels of anti-
Semitism are higher among black Americans than among white
Americans may be spurious. So we shall look at the impact of all of
these other factors: years of formal education, level of political information, size of family income, age, gender, religion, living in the
South, and, in addition, growing up in the South. Obviously, even
taking account of so many factors, there may be still others that
should be included, and every factor we are considering we are
assessing imperfectly, as is always and inescapably the case.[80] Nevertheless, we are doing everything in our power to see if the appearance of higher levels of anti-Semitism among blacks is misleading.
Just so far as this appearance of higher anti-Semitism is due to factors other than race, the differences between black and white views
of Jews will shrink or possibly disappear altogether.

[77] Kuklinski, Cobb, and Gilens 1997.
[78] Glock and Stark 1966.
[79] Ibid.
[80] This is particularly true of religiosity. We only have information as to whether
respondents are Protestant or not, and not the particular Protestant (and fundamentalist) beliefs they do or do not hold.

TABLE 3.2
Predicting Anti-Semitism from Race
(Regression Coefficients)

	Race Only	Other Factors	All Together
Predictors			
Black (versus White)	.16*		.10*
Education		−.10*	−.10*
Psychological Tolerance		.28*	.26*
Political Information		−.11*	−.10*
Age		.10*	.11*
Gender (Male)		.05*	.05*
Live in South		.04*	.05*
Grew Up in South		−.02	−.03
Family Income		−.04	−.03
Protestant		−.01	−.02
Constant	.39	.36	.35
Multiple R	.213	.449	.465
R-squared	.046	.202	.212

Note: $N = 1,824$; *$p < .05$. All of the variables were scaled 0–1.
Source: 1991 Race and Politics Survey.

How can we tell if blacks really are more anti-Semitic than whites given that a variety of other factors may make blacks misleadingly appear to be so? Simultaneously analyzing the responses of black and white Americans from the National Race and Politics Study, we can see if the relation between race and anti-Semitism is genuine or spurious. We proceed in three steps. The first is to estimate the size of the relationship between race and anti-Semitism *disregarding the influence of any other factor*. From the results we have already seen, when we compared black and white levels of agreement with individual stereotypes, we know that black scores on the overall index of anti-Semitism will be higher than white scores. But what we need to obtain is an estimate of how much higher black scores are. The answer is reported in the first column of table 3.2, which shows that the scores of black Americans on the anti-Semitism Index are on average, .16 higher (on a scale from 0 to 1) than those of white Americans.[81]

[81] The values reported are for unstandardized regression coefficients with all variables scored from 0 to 1.

The question of course is how much of this higher score is attributable not to black Americans being black, but to their having had, for example, less opportunity for education and the like. To figure how much is attributable to factors other than race we take a second step and calculate the impact of these other factors on anti-Semitism *disregarding the influence of race*. We want to cover the widest possible range of other factors, and so included are levels of education; amount of family income; personality factors (in accordance with the Index of Psychological Tolerance);[82] region of the country grew up in (South/non-South); age; gender; region of the country live in (South/non-South); religion (Protestant/non-Protestant); and for good measure, political awareness and sophistication (indexed by level of knowledge about politics). This is very much a kitchen-sink approach to analysis, simultaneously throwing in every factor of conceivable relevance without first working through the relation of each to the others. But the goal is simply to take account of every possibly confounding factor we can, and, doing so, we find that the results parallel those of previous research. For example, the less well educated one tends to be, the more hostile and cynical one's psychological make-up, the older, less politically aware, and sophisticated one is, the more anti-Semitic one is likely to be. Anti-Semitic respondents are also more likely to be male and to live in the South.

Although these results are of importance in their own right, what is of overriding importance here is the connection, if any, between being black and a disposition toward anti-Semitism. We therefore take a third step, and see what happens when, to this long list of other factors, race is added.

How much is the impact of being black reduced when the whole gallery of collateral factors is taken into account? If you compare the size of the coefficient for race in columns 1 and 3, you will see the impact of race is indeed reduced—by about 40 percent. This means two things. It means, first, that the apparent contribution of being black to anti-Semitism is overstated when the impact of collateral factors is neglected. But it also means, and this is the second lesson, that even when the impact of these factors is taken into account, race still makes a difference: indeed, the results in table 3.2 suggest

[82] For a detailed account of the history and validation of the measure of Psychological Tolerance, see Sniderman et al. 2000, chap. 3.

that even after the role of education and a host of other factors is eliminated, the level of anti-Semitism still is about .10 higher (on a scale from 0 to 1) among black Americans than among white Americans. It is possible that controlling for additional variables could reduce this difference further, but our data suggest that at least some differences would remain.

Black Anti-Semitism, Black Pride, and the Black Muslims

Does black pride encourage black anti-Semitism? In light of the contested role of Jewish businessmen in inner cities, one could argue that black support for economic autonomy, for example, reinforces anti-Semitism. Perhaps; but it seems a stretch to argue that a desire to play a larger part in the economy of their communities nowadays is the primary engine driving hostility against Jews, and, in any case, the work of Herring and her colleagues has called into question whether there is a connection between ingroup identification and outgroup rejection for blacks.[83] Speaking for ourselves, it is not obvious why feeling a sense of common fate with other blacks or wishing blacks to have a stronger sense of pride and self-respect should encourage hostility to Jews. Afrocentrism, on the other hand, may be another matter. It encourages a suspension of critical standards and readiness to oversimplify—"cognitive simplism," in Selznick and Steinberg's phrase—the same trait that provides a basis for anti-Semitism among white Americans.[84] It is hardly a stretch, therefore, to suggest that a willingness to approve of anti-Semitism may go along with a readiness to accuse whites of culture-theft.

The question of whether black pride is tied to black anti-Semitism can be addressed in different ways. We will look at three, taking advantage of our Chicago survey. The first, and simplest, is to look at the regression coefficients between anti-Semitism and various forms of racial identification one at a time. When you do this calculation, there are two things to observe (column 1 of table 3.3). The first is the modest size of most of these coefficients. This means that,

[83] See Herring, Jankowsi, and Brown 1999. We have learned a great deal from their analysis, even if we disagree with some of the details of their conclusions.

[84] Selznick and Steinberg 1969.

TABLE 3.3
Racial Identification and Anti-Semitism
(Regression Coefficients)

	Alone	Four Racial Identification Measures	Afrocentrism and Conspiratorial Thinking
Predictors			
Autonomy	.13*	.06	
Afrocentrism	.25*	.24*	.14*
Common Fate	.04	−.06	
Build Pride	.04	−.01	
Conspiratorial Thinking			.24*
Multiple R		.276	.362
R-squared		.076	.131

Note: $N = 469$; *$p < .05$. All of the variables were scaled 0–1.

as a general proposition, the tie between anti-Semitism and feelings of racial solidarity is minor. The second is that one particular expression of a sense of racial solidarity, Afrocentrism, is more closely bound up with anti-Semitism than any of the others, although a desire for economic autonomy is also significantly related.

Both observations are technically accurate but also potentially misleading. As we saw in chapter 2, the gallery of forms of black pride tend to go together. Blacks who want more economic autonomy, who feel they share a common fate with other blacks, or who wish to strengthen black pride and self-respect, are more likely to endorse Afrocentric claims than are blacks who attach less importance to these goals. But just insofar as these ideas go together, there is an obvious danger that some may falsely appear to be tied to anti-Semitism, not because there is a genuine association between them, but because they are connected with Afrocentrism, which genuinely is bound up with anti-Semitism. And, in fact, once we take into account the interconnectedness of different forms of racial identification, the link between most forms of black pride and anti-Semitism disappears (column 2 of table 3.3). Only Afrocentrism is significantly related to anti-Semitism; the other forms of racial identification only appear to be related to anti-Semitism because they are related to Afrocentrism.

To overlook this distinction is one risk; but there is a second, more subtle than the first. Afrocentrism itself may appear, falsely, to be tied to anti-Semitism. Afrocentric claims have a conspiratorial flavor to them, with their suggestions, for example, that ancient Greek philosophers knowingly took credit for ideas that belonged to black Egyptian predecessors or that modern science refuses to acknowledge the debt it knows it owes to African wise men. Perhaps it is not Afrocentrism per se, but a penchant for conspiratorial thinking that encourages black anti-Semitism. Certainly, it is not hard to see how a readiness to believe that others—ancient philosophers or modern scientists—have treated you badly could go along with a readiness to believe that Jews treat you badly. And we have seen that a substantial segment of the black community—not a majority, to be sure, but a substantial minority—insists that conspiracies on a larger scale than ever, indeed, more malevolent than ever, are still being carried on. Just so far as African Americans are prepared to believe that their own government is trying to destroy them, it seems a reasonable conjecture that they will be open to the idea that others also wish to harm them, very much including Jews. And just so far as this is true, then perhaps a penchant for conspiratorial thinking, rather then the claims for recognition of black accomplishment that underpin Afrocentrism, is tied to anti-Semitism. However, as we see in column 3 of table 3.3, the relation between Afrocentrism and prejudice is reduced, but it remains significant even taking account of a penchant for conspiratorial thinking, which is itself also significantly related to anti-Semitism.

There are, however, still other currents of thought in the black community beyond Afrocentrism and conspiratorial thinking that encourage black hostility to Jews. Our study focuses on Chicago; and there are obvious grounds for investigating whether the Black Muslims under the leadership of Louis Farrakhan help stimulate resentment and hostility to Jews in the wider black community. Notice there are two elements here: the Black Muslims and Louis Farrakhan. A good place to start is to ask whether the connection between them matters.

As part of our exploration of black thought, we asked our respondents how they felt about a number of famous black leaders. We asked them to rate each figure "on a thermometer that runs from zero to one hundred. The higher the number, the warmer or more favorable you feel toward that person. The lower the number, the colder or less favorable. If you feel neither warm nor cold toward them, rate that person a fifty." "Feeling thermometers," as they are called in the trade, are standard measures, but in assessing how blacks feel about Louis Farrakhan, we added a twist. Farrakhan, we suspected, is a more potent figure, commanding more support in the wider black community, when he is presented in the trappings of his role as leader of the Black Muslims. We put this idea to a simple test. We asked one half of the respondents how they felt about "Louis Farrakhan"; we asked the other half how they felt about "Louis Farrakhan, the head of the Black Muslims." Consistent with our suspicion, Farrakhan is more popular when he is identified as the leader of the Black Muslims. Identified just by name, his average rating on the feeling thermometer is 54 degrees; presented as leader of the Black Muslims, it is 60 (see table 3.4).[85]

This is a result worth thinking about. Many believe—or perhaps more accurately, hope—that the Black Muslims represent a fringe element in the black community. On this optimistic view, their influence, though real enough, is confined to a relatively small number of avowed adherents drawn from the margins of black communities. The boost in Farrakhan's popularity when he is presented in his leadership role suggests otherwise. If the Muslims were broadly disliked and disdained in the black community, the result would have been exactly the other way around. Farrakhan's popularity would have been lower when he was identified as the leader of the Black Muslims. Instead, calling attention to the Black Muslims, rather than lowering his popularity, boosts it, pointing to the power of this group, not just among its inner circle of adherents, but in the wider black community.[86]

In thinking about the significance of this boost to Farrakhan's

[85] We have inspected the result for a variety of response biases. We have found none, but it is worth noting explicitly that the difference between the two experimental conditions is probably *not* the result of a selection effect; the rate of nonresponse (don't know or refuse to answer) does not differ much when Farrakhan is identified as the leader of the Black Muslims (2.1 percent) and when he is identified in his own right (4.7 percent).

[86] We do not want mechanically to repeat that the sample is drawn from Chicago, the national headquarters of the Black Muslims; but since the issue is the standing of the Muslims in the black community, it is worth repeating a warning here that Chicago may be atypical in this respect.

TABLE 3.4
Popularity of Louis Farrakhan and Black Muslims as a Symbol

	Rating of Farrakhan (Means between 0 and 100)
Description of Farrakhan	
Louis Farrakhan	
(No mention of Black Muslims)	54
Louis Farrakhan, the head of the Black Muslims	60

Note: ANOVA test for the difference: $p = .01$. Cell Ns = 364 and 360.

popularity when he is identified as leader of the Black Muslims, we must call attention to the fact that the reference to the Black Muslims is hardly lengthy. On the contrary, it could not have been briefer. And so far from dramatizing the accomplishments or ideology of the Muslims, it was deliberately perfunctory, no more than a mention of their name. Yet the mere mention of their name, cursory though it was, was sufficient to boost Farrakhan's popularity in the wider black community, at least by a few degrees.

Having said this, it is important to place Farrakhan's popularity in comparative perspective. In addition to asking about Farrakhan, we also asked about Martin Luther King, Jr. and Jesse Jackson.[87] King, not surprisingly, stands head and shoulders above both Farrakhan and Jackson. King's (average) rating is an extraordinary 92 out of a possible 100. He retains legendary status. By comparison, Jesse Jackson averages 74 degrees. But if Jackson does not command the same iconic status as King, he clearly enjoys a more favorable reputation than does Farrakhan.

If you are the sort of person inclined to take comfort from this, we are obliged to add a warning. It is true, and not unimportant, that more in the black community dislike Farrakhan (that is, assign him a score of less than 50 degrees) than dislike Jackson.[88] But it also is true, and perhaps as important, that the segment in the wider black

[87] The order in which the three names were presented was randomized in order to eliminate order effects.

[88] Thirty percent dislike Farrakhan if no mention is made of the Black Muslims. If he is described as "the head of the Black Muslims," 17 percent dislike him. By contrast, only 8 percent dislike Jackson.

community who like Farrakhan (that is, assign him a score of more than 50 degrees) is large, indeed—in our sample, nearly half.[89] And, among them, Farrakhan is just as admired as is Jackson for those who give him a positive rating. Specifically, blacks who have a positive view of Farrakhan, that is, rate him over 50 degrees, rate him at a very warm 82 degrees; blacks who rate Jackson over 50 degrees rate him at 84 degrees on average—virtually no difference.[90] Farrakhan *is* a divisive figure. Many in the black community dislike him. But many like him. And those who do like Farrakhan hold him in the same high esteem as do those who like Jackson.

The crucial question of course is whether Farrakhan's popularity in the wider black community carries a price in terms of black intolerance. It is not difficult to cite pronouncements by Farrakhan and his lieutenants that legitimate, or even invite, anti-Semitism. But journalistic evidence notwithstanding, is Farrakhan's popularity in the wider black community in fact tied to hostility toward Jews? In working out an answer, we want to attribute to Farrakhan only the measure of anti-Semitism he may encourage, and avoid attributing to him an extra measure because his popularity is tied to other factors that, independent of him, promote anti-Semitism. Therefore, when calculating the possible impact of Farrakhan on the attitudes of African Americans toward Jews, we shall also take into account the array of established sources of anti-Semitism just examined, and in addition, the impact of some strands of contemporary black thought, such as Afrocentrism and conspiratorial thinking that we have just seen to be tied in some measure to anti-Semitism.

It is important to underline that all we have to work with is one measure of one aspect of African Americans' orientation to Farrakhan: how favorably they say they feel toward him. As a practical matter, having only one measure, and a crude one at that, means that our estimate will underestimate Farrakhan's true impact. Yet notwithstanding the limits of our measure, we still can see that liking Farrakhan makes a difference. The more favorably African

[89] The figure for Farrakhan is 42 percent if no mention is made of the Black Muslims, and 49 percent if the Black Muslims are mentioned. The comparable figure for Jackson is 76 percent. Note that about a third of respondents are neutral (50 degrees) on Farrakhan.

[90] The 95 percent confidence interval of each mean is greater than 1 point in each direction.

TABLE 3.5
Predicting Anti-Semitism from Farrakhan Rating
(Regression Coefficients)

	Basic Set	Add Mention of Black Muslims
Predictors		
Farrakhan Rating	.14*	.12*
Mention of Black Muslims	–	.08*
Afroentrism	.16*	.15*
Conspiratorial Thinking	.14*	.16*
Psychological Tolerance	.30*	.30*
Gender (Male)	.06*	.05*
Education	−.07	−.07
Age	−.09	−.08
Constant	.18	.14
Multiple R	.537	.558
R-squared	.289	.312

Note: N = 479; *p < .05. All of the variables were scaled 0–1.

Americans feel toward Louis Farrakhan, the more anti-Semitic they are likely to be (see the first column of table 3.5). A rough way of conveying the size of this effect is to observe that admiration for Farrakhan makes approximately the same size contribution to anti-Semitism as does a readiness to affirm Afrocentric ideas or to embrace across-the-board racial conspiracies. None of these are the fundamental reasons for anti-Semitism among African Americans. They are important because they boost the anti-Semitism of blacks above the level it would otherwise be, given their social circumstances and individual makeup.[91]

But is it really fair to speak this way? All that we actually know is that liking Farrakhan, for example, is correlated with disliking Jews. The two may be correlated because Farrakhan encourages blacks to dislike Jews. On the other hand, they may be correlated because disliking Jews leads blacks to like Farrakhan. Ordinarily, there is no way to distinguish between the two alternatives. As the catchphrase has

[91] In this estimation, the impact of education becomes insignificant. For an explanation of this effect, see the discussion of the interplay of education, conspiratorial thinking, and Afrocentrism in chapter 2.

it, correlation is not causation. But because our study makes use of randomized experiments, which make it possible to tell what is cause and what is effect, it can throw light on whether Farrakhan and the Black Muslims provoke hostility toward Jews, or merely benefit from it.

Think back to the "Black Muslim" experiment. By "priming" the Black Muslims as a symbol—calling some people's attention to them, but not that of others—we have gotten a glimpse of the Muslims' power to influence thinking in the wider black community: in this case, to evoke a more favorable evaluation of Louis Farrakhan. But reactions to Farrakhan cannot be the only thing that the Muslims have the power to influence. And one matter with which the Black Muslims are closely identified is their stance toward Jews. Over the years, Black Muslim spokesmen have leveled a stream of highly publicized, highly controversial accusations against Jews— against Jews in business, against Jews in Hollywood and the media generally, against Jewish union leaders, Jewish educators, Jewish financiers, and Jewish politicians.

Given the number of anti-Semitic incidents, memories of them tend to blur. It may be useful, therefore, to recall an example of Black Muslim rhetoric to restore an appreciation of its venom. In New York City's Madison Square Garden, on October 7, 1985, Farrakhan delivered a bitingly anti-Semitic speech. "The Jewish lobby," he declared, "has a stranglehold on the government of the United States."[92] Then, playing to his audience, he asked rhetorically, "Who were the enemies of Jesus?" "Jews! Jews! Jews!," they chanted in response. Then, responding to their chant, Farrakhan declared: "Jesus had a controversy with the Jews. Farrakhan had a controversy with the Jews. Jesus was hated by the Jews. Farrakhan is hated by the Jews. Jesus was scourged by Jews in their temple. Farrakhan is scourged by Jews in their synagogues." Finally, referring again to Jews, he said, "The scriptures charge your people with killing the prophets of God," and, "I am your last chance, Jews"; it will be too late "when God puts you in the oven." The audience's response, according to an on-the-scene reporter, was roaring agreement.

The Madison Square Garden speech of course is only one of a number of anti-Semitic incidents involving Farrakhan, and Far-

[92] See Dinnerstein 1994, pp. 220–21.

rakhan himself is only one of a number of Black Muslims who have made viciously anti-Semitic charges. Again we limit ourselves to one instance. Steve Cokely, a disciple of Farrakhan and an aide to Eugene Sawyer, then acting mayor of Chicago, publicly declared that Jewish doctors injected the AIDS virus into black babies and that Jews were involved in a conspiracy to take over the world.[93] It seems safe to say that the Black Muslims, if they have had an impact, have strengthened rather than weakened negative stereotypes of Jews in the black community.

Thinking of these expressions of Black Muslim anti-Semitism suggested the last step of the analysis. Priming Black Muslims had led our black respondents to think more favorably of Louis Farrakhan. Would it lead them to think less favorably of Jews? To determine whether calling attention to the Black Muslims stimulates a more hostile response to Jews, we first calculated the impact of all of the factors we have considered to this point, then added, as a final consideration, whether the attention of respondents was called to the Black Muslims or not (again, see the second column of table 3.5). As you can see, those whose attention was explicitly called to the Muslims are more likely to endorse negative stereotypes of Jews than those to whom no mention was made of Muslims. The effect is not a large one, but it is both a statistically and substantively significant one.

We want to say quite directly that we were taken aback by this result. The idea that the Muslims might provoke hostility to Jews was in no way surprising. What did surprise us was the persistence of the experimental effect. The priming of Black Muslims took place near the beginning of the interview. Since no mention was subsequently made of the Muslims, the only people who had their attention called to the Black Muslims are those who were randomly assigned to be exposed to the treatment condition. But the assessment of negative stereotypes of Jews took place some ten minutes later. One would think that more than enough time had passed for the experimental effect to have faded, and so we performed a variety of cross-checks, examining all of the potential confounding effects (for example, differences in education or psychological tolerance) that we could think of, without finding any.

---

[93] The characterization of Cokely's charges is Dinnerstein's. See p. 221.

It also is worth remembering that one reason we picked Chicago as a site for our study is precisely because it is the headquarters city for Louis Farrakhan's Black Muslims. It is not unreasonable to believe that the Muslims have a more visible presence and a greater importance there than in other cities. And it is possible, therefore, that the link we have observed there between support for Farrakhan and the Black Muslims may not appear elsewhere. But without minimizing the importance of testing all of our results on further samples, we should be much surprised if the connections we have observed between Afrocentrism and conspiratorial thinking, on the one side, and anti-Semitism, on the other, were not to prove robust.

To step back from the details of these analyses, our most important finding is that black pride and black prejudice tend to be independent of one another. With the exception of Afrocentrism, blacks who attach the most importance to ideas of racial pride and solidarity are neither more likely, nor less likely, to be anti-Semitic than those who attach less importance to these ideas. This finding should comfort many who have worried, not without cause, about the temptations of group loyalty. But if you reflect on our results to this point, you will see that they are incomplete. It is one thing to react to another group as a general proposition. It is another to react to them in the face of a clash between members of that group and members of your own. And in the face of a conflict between a Jew and a black, even blacks who express a positive attitude toward Jews in the abstract may react quite negatively in such circumstances.

When blacks and Jews clash, do feelings of racial pride and solidarity lead blacks to rally against Jews? Does hostility toward Jews lead blacks who are prejudiced to take up a banner of loyalty to fellow blacks? Under the pressure of group conflict, do ingroup loyalty and outgroup hostility become opposite sides of the same coin?

Conflict between Jews and Blacks: The "College Editor" Experiment

Many commentators, expert and otherwise, are persuaded that a gulf of misunderstanding has opened up between black

Americans and Jewish Americans.[94] Many blacks and Jews, though no doubt more of the latter than of the former, believe that blacks have lost the sympathy they once may have felt for Jews because of Jewish support for the civil rights movement. Indeed, it is impossible to miss in the voices of some black activists a suggestion of Jewish desertion, even of Jewish betrayal, of the civil rights movement, just as it is impossible to miss in the judgments of other commentators, by no means all of them Jewish, a suggestion that blacks are perfectly prepared to condone an act if done by a black that they would be all too quick to condemn if performed by a Jew. But all that is available to decide the truth or falsity of these claims are the views of activists. How ready are those who make up the black community as a whole to practice a double standard when it comes to Jews? If it is true, is it true of only a small number? Or is it true, as many fear, of a large number?

To throw some light on these questions, we conducted the "College Editor" experiment. The objective of the experiment is to see whether blacks will treat criticism of blacks by a Jew the same as criticism of Jews by a black. The experiment begins by informing all of our respondents that the next questions are about what they think should be done about some controversial issues. Then, half the time, the interviewer says:

> Suppose the Jewish editor of a college newspaper was fired for printing an article that criticized black students on campus. How do you feel about firing the editor? Are you in favor of, or opposed to, firing the editor?

Here are the essential elements of a classic confrontation over race. Blacks are subjected to criticism. In turn, they see the other as possibly racist, and racially insensitive at the least. So in the College Editor experiment it is not difficult to imagine that black Americans may feel that the Jewish editor has overstepped the bounds of what is proper, either because they are concerned about the respect due to a fellow black, or because they dislike Jews, or both.

The other half of the time, by contrast, the positions of Jews and blacks are precisely reversed. The interviewer says.

[94] See, for example, Berman 1994; Franklin, Grant, Kletnick, and McNeil 1998; Lerner and West 1995.

> Suppose the black editor of a college newspaper was fired for printing an article that criticized Jewish students on campus. How do you feel about firing the editor? Are you in favor of, or opposed to, firing the editor?

This second scenario, with a black at the center of a storm of controversy, in need of support from fellow blacks, should be as immediately familiar and convincing to our black respondents as the first. The scenario of a black under attack, and in need of support from fellow blacks, has been played out many times. Will African Americans rally around the editor out of a sense of solidarity and loyalty to a fellow black? Will they defend him, whether or not they feel a sense of pride in being black, because they do not like Jews?

Notice a pair of advantages of experimental randomization. First, in a standard public opinion interview, all of the respondents would have been asked about both the Jewish and the black editors. But then, whatever the order in which the questions about the two editors are asked, people's answer to the first may constrain their answer to the second. If they are asked first about the black editor, and respond that he should *not* be fired, they are under pressure to take the same position with the Jewish editor, or risk creating an impression that they are intolerant. Alternatively, if they are asked first about the Jewish editor, and respond that he should be fired, they are under pressure to take the same position with the black editor, or risk creating an impression that they are unprincipled. This dilemma is sidestepped by asking them about either one or the other, but not both. Second, since the choice of whether they are asked whether the Jewish or the black editor should be fired was made on a random basis, and since everything in the two versions of the question is otherwise identical, just so far as our black respondents are readier to say that the Jewish editor should be fired, we can infer that they are practicing a double standard.

How serious is the problem of black favoritism, of a double standard in making judgments about blacks and about Jews, not in the abstract, but rather in the context of a specific controversy? The answer, the results of the College Editor experiment suggest, is quite remarkable. As you can see in figure 3.5, 41 percent of our black respondents feel that the Jewish editor should be fired; by comparison, 37 percent believe that the black editor should be fired. This is

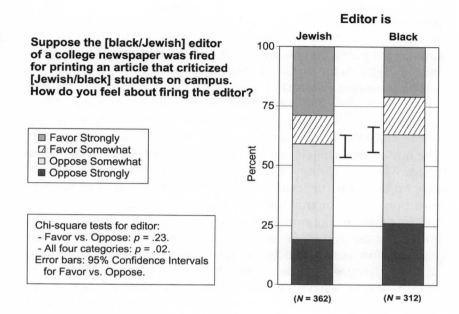

Figure 3.5. Firing College Editor

a difference, but only a slight one; indeed, so slight a one as to fail to be statistically, let alone substantively, significant. Without wishing to strike rhetorical flourishes, we cannot think of many who have followed the strain between blacks and Jews in America over the last generation who would have predicted this degree of even-handedness.

Yet it is also clear from the figure that blacks more strongly favor firing the Jewish editor and more strongly oppose firing the black editor. An obvious candidate for explaining this difference in intensity of reactions is the appeal of racial pride and solidarity. It may seem no more than common sense that the more importance that blacks attach to black pride, the more likely they are to treat a person caught up in racial conflict differently depending on whether he is black or not. This may happen in two ways. However they feel about the Jewish editor, blacks may be more reluctant to fire the black editor the more they feel a sense of identification with other blacks; and the more, therefore, they wish to rally to his defense. Alternatively, however they feel about the black editor, they may be readier to fire the Jewish editor the more importance they attach to racial pride; and the more, therefore, they are inclined to take umbrage at publication of an article critical of blacks. Which possibility is right, or are both—or is neither?

The unspoken fear is that black pride fans the fires of black-Jewish conflicts. We believe that both black and white commentators share this fear, though, as with any matter where people do not feel free to voice their true opinions, it is difficult to be certain this is so. The findings are therefore worth stating in the clearest possible language. The first column of table 3.6 shows the correlations between support for firing the Jewish editor and various forms of racial identification.[95] It is true that the more committed black respondents are to Afrocentrism, the more likely they are to favor firing the Jewish editor. But this is the only form of racial identification that has any impact. How committed blacks are to economic autonomy; how strongly they feel a sense of common fate with other blacks; how important they believe it is to build black pride and self-respect—all are quite irrelevant to their view of whether the Jewish editor should or should not be fired.

The second column of table 3.6 reports the correlations between the various forms of racial identification and support for firing the black editor. There are several things to note. First, although Afrocentrism inclines blacks to favor firing the Jewish editor, it does not dispose them to rally around the black editor. In a word, Afrocentrism encourages rejection of the outgroup, but, in this case, it does not encourage identification with the ingroup. Second, two forms of racial identification do encourage blacks to rally around the black editor: support for economic autonomy and support for building black pride and self-respect. But remember that both were irrelevant to whether blacks believed that the Jewish editor should be fired. In short, both of these two forms of racial identification encourage blacks to identify with their group but do *not* encourage them to reject others.

That some forms of black pride reinforce black loyalty should not be surprising. Nor problematic. There is nothing intrinsically repre-

---

[95] We show the zero-order correlations, so that the relation between each form of racial identification and support for firing the editor can be seen, without the relations of any being minimized by the tendency of shared variance to be apportioned to the primary predictors in multiple regression.

TABLE 3.6
Racial Identification and Double Standards
(Correlation Coefficients)

	Correlation between Racial Identification and Favor Firing College Editor if Editor is:	
	Jewish	*Black*
Racial Identification		
Autonomy	.06	−.20*
Afrocentrism	.15*	−.03
Common Fate	.02	−.07
Build Pride	.04	−.15*
(Number)	(257)	(231)

Note: *p < .05.

hensible in this. The more strongly anyone identifies with a group—black, Jewish, or another—the more likely he or she is to come to the assistance of a fellow group member. The moral concern over black pride is different. It has to do, not with helping someone who is black because he is black, but turning against someone who is not black because he is not black.

Against the background of this concern, the results of the College Editor experiment are striking. A desire for more autonomy for blacks, or for building more pride and self-respect among blacks, does encourage blacks to rally in defense of a fellow black. But neither encourages blacks in any significant degree to call for the firing of the Jewish editor. This is a result worth emphasizing. For it means that, with the exception of Afrocentrism, which is an exception at many points, considerations of racial pride strengthen identification with the ingroup *without strengthening rejection of the outgroup*. Black pride encourages blacks to rally around fellow blacks without encouraging them to react against Jews.

Black pride, however, is only part of the story. The other obvious part is black anti-Semitism. It cannot be surprising that if blacks dislike Jews, they are much more likely to favor firing the Jewish editor for criticizing blacks students than firing the black editor for criticizing Jewish students, though it may be a little surprising just how

TABLE 3.7
Black Anti-Semitism and Black Double Standards
(Means Favoring Firing Editor 0–1 and Standard Errors)

	Favor Firing College Editor if Editor is: (Means 0–1 and Standard Errors)	
	Jewish	Black
Anti-Semitism		
High	.68 (.04)	.33 (.03)
Middle	.48 (.03)	.50 (.04)
Low	.39 (.03)	.51 (.04)
(Minimum cell N)	(100)	(86)

Note: ANOVA tests:
–Effect of Anti-Semitism: $p = .18$.
–Effect of Jewish versus Black Editor: $p = .02$.
–Interaction effect: $p < .01$.

large a difference anti-Semitism makes. If you look at the reactions of, say, the most negative third of blacks (see the first row of table 3.7), you will see that they are more likely to favor firing the Jewish editor by a factor of two to one. What is more, if they are in favor of firing, they are significantly more likely to be strongly in favor of firing the Jewish editor than the black editor.

It would be a mistake to minimize the importance of this result on the grounds that it is what one would expect. For it makes plain why black anti-Semitism is a matter of concern. It is not, as is sometimes suggested, merely symbolic posturing, empty rhetoric without significance for how people actually react to conflicts between blacks and others. What the College Editor experiment shows is that, when blacks and Jews come into conflict, the animus that many blacks feel for Jews in general gets translated into a hostile, punitive reaction against individual Jews.

But the experiment also shows something else: something more surprising. We have just looked at those blacks with the most negative attitudes toward Jews. If you look now at those with the most positive attitudes toward Jews (bottom row of table 3.7), you will see that they are more likely to favor firing the *black* editor than the Jewish editor. This may strike you as too much of a good thing—blacks being more willing to rally around a Jew than a fellow black. For our part, while we did not feel it had to turn out this way, it seems to us understandable that it could. The blacks here have been identified as having positive attitudes towards Jews. They do not have a specific reason for lining up in defense of the black editor—and indeed they divide about equally over what should happen to him. But they have, because their attitudes toward Jews are relatively positive, a specific reason for supporting the Jewish editor.

We understand why some may be skeptical that (any group of) blacks would rally to the support of a Jew even more readily than to the support of a fellow black. In the last experiment in this chapter, the "Allegations of Racism" experiment, we therefore return to the question of whether (a substantial number of) blacks feel a special affinity with Jews. It may go too far to say that the results of this final experiment clinch the findings of this one. But they do strengthen them.

Prejudice and Group Loyalty:
The Immigrant Tax Burden Experiment

Dislike members of another group and you obviously will be disposed to react against them. This is straightforward. What is less obvious is whether if you dislike another group it will dispose you to rally around your own group. In the College Editor experiment, we saw that black anti-Semitism fuels hostility to the Jewish editor and also support for the black editor. But in the experiment, of course, the black editor has published an article critical of Jewish students. Hostility to Jews and support for a black are thus fused together in the experimental situation. In supporting the black editor one is simultaneously supporting criticism of Jews: it cannot be surprising that doing so should appeal to blacks who dislike Jews.

For our part, we are skeptical that black anti-Semitism promotes black solidarity. We believe that the proposition that prejudice toward an outgroup in general promotes loyalty to the ingroup represents a misreading of the psychology of intolerance. At its core, prejudice involves an indiscriminate readiness to dislike and derogate others.[96] This indiscriminateness is the signature feature of big-otry.[97] And an indiscriminate readiness to dislike others is not a nat-ural breeding ground for loyalty, a feeling of affinity, or a sense of trust. On the contrary, as a growing body of studies have shown, outgroup hostility is unrelated to ingroup loyalty under many con-ditions, and just so far as prejudice involves an overreadiness to rejects others, we expect that hostility to the outgroup should most commonly go along with hostility, not loyalty, to the ingroup.[98]

To see whether this is so or not, we carried out the "Immigrant Tax Burden" experiment. The question text runs as follows:

> Many different groups of people have come to the United States at different times in history. In recent years, the number of [here the name of a particular immigrant group is men-tioned] has been increasing. How likely do you think it is that the growing number of [the name of the immigrant group is mentioned again] will cause taxes to increase because they will need more public services? Would you say it is very likely, somewhat likely, not too likely, or not at all likely?

To see whether it matters whether the immigrants are black or not, a random third of the time the immigrant group is identified as "Mexicans and other Hispanics;" one-third of the time as "Koreans and other Asians;" and one-third as "immigrants from countries in Africa."

It is no secret that the popular culture, black or white, does not strongly discourage negative views about immigration. Our respon-dents certainly are quite willing to express negative views of immi-grants, whatever country they are from. Thus, about two-thirds of respondents say that it is at least somewhat likely that immigrants "will cause taxes to increase because they will need more public ser-vices" (figure 3.6). But there is a harder edge to their views about Latino or Asian immigrants. If you compare their reactions to immi-grants from different countries, you will see that our black respon-

---

[96] For a discussion of alternative conceptualizations of prejudice and a justification of one centered on consistency of negative affect, see Sniderman et al. 2000, chap. 2.

[97] To cite an example, it is Italians who most dislike immigrants who are the most likely to dislike other Italians: from the North if they are from the South, from the South if they are from the North. See Sniderman et al. 2000, chap. 3.

[98] See especially Brewer 2001.

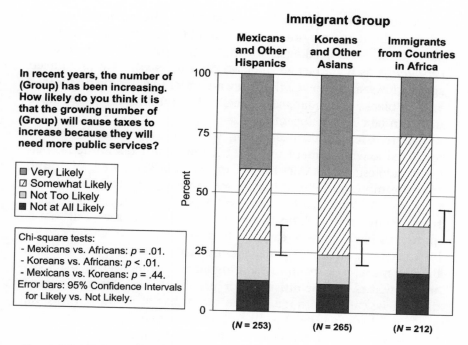

Figure 3.6. Immigrant Tax Burden

dents are significantly more likely to believe that Mexicans and other Hispanics, and Koreans and other Asians, will bring about an increase in taxes than to believe that immigrants from countries in Africa will do the same.

The crucial question, however, is whether black prejudice promotes black solidarity. And to answer this question, we have to look not at how blacks in general respond, but rather at how those who are prejudiced react. This question has two parts. The first is, if blacks are prejudiced against a particular group, say, Jews, does this bear on how they will react to Asians and Latinos? Notice the differences, certainly, between Jews and Latinos. It used to be common, when one wanted to give a sympathetic gloss to black anti-Semitism, to point to the dominating role of Jewish merchants in inner-city ghettoes. The same justification cannot be mustered for black hostility to Latinos. But notwithstanding the many points of difference between Jews and Latinos, the first of the modern studies of prejudice, *The Authoritarian Personality*, taught us that those who are prejudiced against one outgroup tend to be systematically more likely to be prejudiced against other outgroups.[99] *The Authoritarian Personality*, as it happened, focused on whites who are prejudiced against Jews, and showed that they are more likely to be prejudiced against blacks and Asians also. The indiscriminateness of prejudice has been labeled ethnocentrism.

It is hard to think of a reason why ethnocentrism should be restricted to white Americans, and the Immigrant Tax Burden experiment suggests that it does indeed apply to blacks, as well. We found that the more prejudiced blacks are against Jews, the more likely they are to declare that Hispanic and Asian immigrants will increase the tax burden on U.S. taxpayers. The effect is not large; but that is quite possibly because a readiness to believe that immigrants carry a big price tag is already prevalent in the black community as a whole. But the moral is worth underscoring all the same. Among blacks as among whites, anti-Semitism is not just about Jews. The readiness to dislike Jews carries with it a readiness to dislike other minorities and, as we shall see, whites, too. It follows that many groups, not just Jews, have a stake in the level of black anti-Semitism.

Another question concerns how the more prejudiced blacks react, not to those who are not black, but to those who are. Does black prejudice lead to black loyalty? We saw in the College Editor experiment that the more anti-Semitic blacks are, the more likely they are to oppose firing the black editor who published an article critical of Jewish students. But of course this result is ambiguous. They may oppose firing the black editor out of loyalty to a fellow black. Alternatively, they may oppose firing him out of hostility to Jews. The Immigrant Tax Burden experiment allows us to distinguish these two possibilities by observing how blacks react to fellow blacks when no other group is involved. If black prejudice really does encourage solidarity with other blacks, then the more prejudiced blacks should be more likely to feel a sense of sympathy and solidarity with immigrants from Africa because they are from Africa.

The results from the Immigrant Tax Burden experiment suggest two further lessons (see table 3.8). First, African Americans who are prejudiced against Jews are significantly more likely to believe that

[99] Adorno, Frenkel-Brunswick, Levinson, and Sanford 1950.

TABLE 3.8
Effect of Anti-Semitism and Building Black Pride on African Immigrant
Tax Burden
(Means from 0 to 1 and Standard Errors)

	Taxes Likely to Increase (Means 0–1 and standard errors)
Anti-Semitism	
High	.62 (.04)
Middle	.69 (.04)
Low	.49 (.04)
Build Pride	
High	.49 (.04)
Low	.63 (.03)
(Minimum cell *N*)	(53)

Note: ANOVA tests:
–Effect of Anti-Semitism: $p < .01$.
–Effect of Build Pride: $p < .01$.

fellow blacks from Africa will cause taxes to increase than are African Americans who are not anti-Semitic.[100] That is to say, blacks who react negatively to Jews are more likely to react negatively to their fellow blacks. Second, blacks who believe it is important to build black pride and black self-respect are markedly less likely to respond negatively to fellow blacks from Africa than are those who do not believe it is important. In short, taking pride in your group encourages you to feel a common bond with other members of your group. But, and this is the point specially conveyed by the Immigrant Tax Burden experiment, disliking another group does not encourage you to value your own.

Charges of White Racism

Arguably the most visible, certainly one of the most distressing, signs of strain between black Americans and white Americans is a steady stream of allegations of white racism. Racism per-

[100] Prejudiced blacks respond even more negatively to Hispanic and Asian immigrants than to immigrants from Africa.

sists. It remains a genuine obstacle in the lives of many blacks to making their way forward and enjoying a full measure of equality. But a charge of racism has itself become a weapon in arguments over race—a potent weapon, as the frequency with which it is brandished has made plain.

How easily, how indiscriminately, a charge of racism can be leveled against someone may not be evident even to those who follow politics with attention. There is something to be gained, therefore, by calling to mind some specific incidents. We rely here on a recent chronicle by John McWhorter. "In January 1999," he relates, "David Howard, the white ombudsman to the newly elected mayor of Washington, D.C., Anthony Williams, casually said in a budget meeting with two coworkers, 'I will have to be niggardly with this money because it's not going to be a lot of money.' One of the two coworkers was black, and left the meeting, charging Howard with racism. A storm erupted. The mayor accepted Howard's resignation. The word 'niggardly' of course has no connection with race. It means stingy, and "it has been used in English," McWhorter, a professor of linguistics relates, "since the Middle Ages, when black people of any kind were unknown in England, and had been imported to the country by Scandinavian Viking invaders in the 800s, in whose tongue *nig* meant 'miser.'"[101] The charge of white racism nonetheless stuck.

Consider a second example. In 1991, at a meeting of black students at Stanford University, a black undergraduate charged "that a white mathematics professor had told her to withdraw from a calculus course because black people were not good at math."[102] McWhorter, himself an African American, was present when the young woman spoke. He observes that it is extremely improbable that the young woman's charges against the professor are valid for reasons that should be obvious to everyone in that room. As he writes, "the chances are nil that anyone with the mental equipment to obtain a professorship at Stanford University would, in the late 1980s in as politicized an atmosphere as an elite university, blithely tell a black student that black people cannot do math. Even if he were of this opinion, he would have to have been brain-dead to

[101] McWhorter 2000, p. vii.
[102] McWhorter, p. 4.

casually throw it into a black student's face, possibly risking his job, reputation, and career."[103]

The only way to assess specific charges of racism is to determine the specific facts of the matter. Here we are interested in a readiness to issue blanket charges of racism. Our concern is the willingness of some blacks to allege that whole categories of people—not this or that white, but whites in general—are biased against blacks. A number of questions need to be asked about this. How prevalent is a readiness to issue blanket charges of racism? Is it fairly rare? Or is it commonplace? And, rare or commonplace, what lies behind it?

In thinking about the issue of blacks' views of whites, we found ourselves thinking again of the place of Jews in the black mind. One reason that blacks may dislike Jews, so far as they do dislike them, is because Jews are white and by any standard whites loom larger in the consciousness of blacks in contemporary America than do Jews. This suggested to us the idea that however much suspicion and hostility African Americans harbor toward Jews, they harbor still more toward whites in general. To test this intuition, we carried out the "Blanket Charges of Racism" experiment. We asked one half of the sample, randomly selected, whether "most whites are racist." We asked the other half whether "most Jews are racist." In both cases, four options are open: to agree strongly, to agree somewhat, to disagree somewhat, to disagree strongly.

How common is a readiness to charge racism? And however common or uncommon it may be, are African Americans more likely to charge whites with racism than to charge Jews, or is it, possibly, the other way around? The first thing to note is that most blacks in our sample *reject* (at least somewhat) blanket charges of racism, whether against whites or Jews (figure 3.7). This, again, is a result worth emphasizing. Our sense is that many observers, black as well as white, are afraid that a large majority of blacks are ready to make blanket charges of racism. We are not suggesting that to have this concern is unreasonable. We are suggesting that, reasonable or not, it is false. And yet, we also must observe that the number of blacks who are ready to issue a blanket charge of racism is very far from trivial. On the order of about one in every four or five are ready to declare that *most* whites and Jews are basically racist. That is a

[103] Ibid.

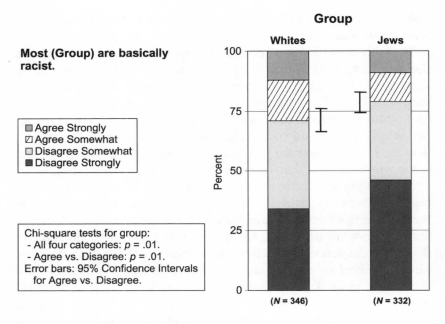

Figure 3.7. Whites/Jews Basically Racist

minority. It is a quite substantial one, however, and corresponds to the finding of Sigelman and Welch, who report in their pathbreaking study that about one in every four blacks perceive that most whites "personally share the attitudes of the Ku Klux Klan toward blacks"—an example of parallel results that cross-validates both studies.[104]

But what about the question of whether African Americans are more likely to charge whites or Jews with racism? If you look at figure 3.7, you will see that blacks are indeed more likely to charge whites than Jews with racism: 29 percent say that whites are basically racist; 21 percent say that Jews are. The difference between these two numbers is statistically significant, but the difference is not a large one, and it is not obvious that in substantive terms it is an important one.

Getting a sense of how ready blacks are to charge others with being racist is only one part of the problem. It is just as important to figure out what lies behind the readiness to issue blanket charges of

[104] See Sigelman and Welch 1991, table 3.1, p. 53.

racism. There are at least two obvious explanatory candidates. The first is racial solidarity. The general intuition here is that identification with the ingroup encourages rejection of the outgroup: the more blacks feel a sense of racial identity and solidarity with other blacks the readier they will be to perceive others who are not black, very much including Jews, as biased against blacks. It is not clear how many believe that having a sense of racial identity or solidarity is a root cause of a readiness to charge racism. It is quite clear, however, that a large number of whites fear that it is.

The second factor that may account for why some blacks believe that Jews in particular are racist is of course anti-Semitism. The intuition here is straightforward. Thinking ill of others does not incline you to think that they will think well of you. Believe that a group of people is reprehensible and you give yourself a reason to believe that they are badly disposed toward you. Believe that they are badly disposed toward you, and you give yourself a reason to believe that they are reprehensible. Either way, blacks who are prejudiced against Jews should find it easy to believe that Jews are prejudiced against them.

How important are considerations of racial pride in encouraging African Americans to charge Jews with racism? Quite remarkably, if you look at table 3.9, you will see that there is no overlap between how committed African Americans are to racial pride in any of the forms that we have considered and how ready they are to say that Jews are racist. This is true for all of the expressions of racial pride we have examined—the desire for autonomy, support for Afrocentrism, a sense of sharing a common fate with other blacks, and a commitment to building black pride and self-respect. The only correlation that is statistically significant is with autonomy, and that correlation is negative, not positive. We believe that the absence of a connection between the appeal of black pride and a readiness to charge Jews with racism is a finding of the first order of importance.

And what about anti-Semitism? Notice that the question is whether blacks who are anti-Semitic are more likely to believe that Jews are prejudiced against them. It cannot be surprising that the answer is yes. Being prejudiced against a group and believing that this group is prejudiced against you go hand-in-hand. This is just as common sense would suggest.

But doesn't this suggest that the basis of blacks' reactions to whites in general will be different? After all, when it comes to white

TABLE 3.9
Correlates of Charging Jews as Being Racist
(Correlation Coefficients)

	Coefficients
Correlates	
Autonomy	−.16*
Afrocentrism	−.07
Common Fate	−.07
Build Pride	−.01
Anti-Semitism	.50*

Note: N = 243; *p < .05.

racism, there is the reality of the American treatment of African Americans—the century and more of slavery, followed by a century and more of state-mandated discrimination and socially approved exploitation. And for all the progress in the last half-century, who would argue that prejudice and discrimination have vanished in white America? Then, too, the persistence of white racism is a prominent topic in black media. And if everyday impressions are a guide, the more committed black media outlets are to celebrating black pride and racial solidarity, the more prominent the discussion of the intractability of prejudice and discrimination. Given all of this, shouldn't we expect that the more committed blacks are to the banner of black pride and racial solidarity, the more responsive they will be to the message of white racism?

It may seem reasonable to believe that black pride stokes a readiness to focus on the racial culpability of whites, to see them as racist. But when this belief is put to an empirical test (table 3.10), it turns out to be wrong. Feelings of racial solidarity, in fact, have scarcely anything to with a readiness to charge that whites are racist. The connection between believing that most whites are racist and feeling that it is important to build black pride, or Afrocentrism, or a desire for autonomy is not statistically significant. And the connection between believing that most whites are racist and sharing a sense of common fate with other blacks is negative—blacks who feel a bond with other blacks are less, not more, likely to perceive whites as racist.

We understand the common presumption that being attached to the flag of black pride encourages blacks to charge that whites as a whole are racist. Before we did these calculations, this seemed to us, though not a sure thing, a very reasonable bet. Not that we expected

TABLE 3.10
Correlates of Charging Whites as Being Racist
(Correlation Coefficients)

	Coefficients
Correlates	
Autonomy	.10
Afrocentrism	.01
Common Fate	−.14*
Build Pride	.05
Anti-Semitism	.33*

Note: N = 254; *p < .05.

that every form of racial pride necessarily would fuel charges of racism. But we could see, for example, how Afrocentrism, with its claims of cultural theft, could encourage a stereotypical judgment of whites as racists. But, our results indicate, it does not; nor does a desire for more autonomy; nor a feeling of solidarity with other blacks; nor a desire to increase black self-respect. Black pride, it appears, has little, if anything, to do with blanket allegations of white racism.

But, then, what does? We just saw that the more prejudiced blacks were against Jews, the more likely they are to believe that Jews are prejudiced against them. This observation may seem tautological. Who should be more likely to think that Jews are racist than those who think ill of Jews across-the-board? But it points to a genuine lesson. The images that people have of what others are like are in significant measure a product of what they themselves are like. Why if people dislike Jews are they very likely to think that Jews dislike them? Because the psychological mechanism of projection is so obviously engaged. The suspicion, hostility, and stereotyping that they themselves feel toward Jews they attribute to Jews. Projection tends to be a general process. And just so far as it is general, it implies that one reason why blacks believe that whites are prejudiced is because they themselves are prejudiced.

To see whether this implication is true, we have carried out a test. Just so far as a readiness to perceive whites as prejudiced is a reflection of blacks themselves being prejudiced, then the more prejudiced blacks are the more likely they should be to say that whites are racist. To make this test a tough one, and eliminate any suggestion of tautology, when we refer to blacks as prejudiced, we shall mean prejudiced against Jews, not against whites.

Is there a connection between blacks saying that whites are prejudiced and being prejudiced themselves? Look at the last correlation (.33) in table 3.10. It shows that the more likely blacks are to charge whites with racism, the more anti-Semitic they themselves are likely to be. This is a result worth reflection. We have seen that only a minority of blacks are ready to charge whites as a whole with racism. But it is a sizeable minority. And the charge of racism, hurled about in public, has become part of the contemporary rhetorical landscape. The lesson of our findings is therefore worth underscoring. For our results show that the quicker blacks are to charge racism the more likely they are themselves to be racist.

Reprise

There are many currents of thought in the contemporary black community. Some flow in a common direction. Some run in different, even conflicting, directions. In this chapter alone, we have seen, among other things, that blacks, so far from fighting over the benefits of affirmative action, are remarkably evenhanded in supporting it, whether it is set up to benefit blacks or not; that they are markedly more anti-Semitic than whites, in part because of sentiments that have gained currency in the black community, like Afrocentrism and a penchant for conspiratorial thinking; that a sense of pride in being black and a feeling of solidarity with other blacks does *not* encourage blacks to react negatively toward Jews—even when, as in the College Editor experiment, it is a matter of a Jew publishing an article critical of black students; and that, as the Charges of Racism experiment showed, the readier blacks are to charge whites with racism, the more likely they are themselves to be racist.

We have focused on black Americans' sense of distinctiveness as blacks and on the extent to which their reactions to other Americans—Jews, Asians, Latinos, and whites—hinge on this sense of distinctiveness. Now we want to consider the view of black Americans toward America itself: its core values, the terms under which they believe they can and should take part, the opportunities they believe it offers, the extent to which they wish to embrace their larger identity as Americans.

F or white Americans, equality is an idea without shadows. It is a value in its own right. It also is of value as a means, indeed arguably *the* means, to achieve equality for blacks.[105] From the perspective of black Americans, the politics of equality looks different. An ironic contradiction is inherent.

It may sound like an exaggeration to speak of a contradiction, ironic or otherwise, as though black Americans somehow are ambivalent about whether equality is what they really want. They are not. Accepting less than equality is not acceptable. But the terms in which the struggle for equality is conducted carry different implications for black and for white Americans.

Consider the idea of integration—say, in its historically quintessential context, the integration of public schools. White or black, if you were committed to equality in the 1950s, you were committed to integration of public schools. Jim Crow systems, one set of schools for whites, another for blacks, had to be overturned. Racially segregated schools were inherently unequal, inescapably discriminatory. Black and white opinion—or, at any rate, liberal white opinion—joined together in support of dismantling segregated schools. But if you were black, the issue of school integration had a sting that it did not have if you were white, however racially liberal a white you were. Why must black school children sit alongside white children if they were to have an equal educational opportunity? Because, to cite a common argument for integration, "through in-

---

[105] We don't mean that the ideas of white Americans about equality are free from internal tension. You have only to think about Blackman's injunction that it is necessary to take race into account in order to go beyond it. But there is no side of the idea of equality that, for whites, is invidious in the way it can be for blacks.

struction by better (predominantly white) teachers and classroom contact with their white peers, who should outnumber them, minority pupils will experience what is tantamount to a personality change by absorbing the achievement-related values of the higher-achieving whites and will thus start achieving themselves."[106] Integration, so advertised, says that black children benefit from sitting alongside white children, nothing of white children who gain from sitting alongside black children; black children need to practice more conscientiously the core values of the larger society, but not white children, whose role instead is to serve as models for their black classmates. There is a double sting here. Blacks have to become more like whites, and to accomplish this, they are dependent on whites and must give up control of historically black institutions.[107]

Either suggestion—that black Americans need to become more like white Americans or that they need white Americans in order to become who they are capable of becoming—has provoked advocates of black nationalism. But to suppose that the idea of common ground is highly charged just for black nationalists misses the deeper irony. In an older view, color blindness stood for an ideal that, however difficult it may be to achieve, represents the ultimate goal to which black and white Americans should be striving. Now, the argument runs, color blindness is arguably the principal "barrier to inclusion."[108]

The new argument against the older ideal of color blindness rests on two premises. One is an empirical claim: that in the absence of recognition of their distinctive culture and identity, black and minority students do not do as well in school as they otherwise would. The other is a normative claim, and it would be pressed whether or not the empirical claim of barriers to achievement were to stand or fall. For, on this new view, what white Americans mean by being color-blind is being blind to any color other than white. Blacks and minorities must "assimilate to the culture, standards, styles of the societal . . . mainstream, while the mainstream . . . [is] not required to take an interest in, or value any of the distinguishing characteristics of, the corresponding features of minority

---

[106] Gerard 1988, p. 230.

[107] For a sensitive exploration of the accomplishments and ambiguities of school integration, see Patterson 2001.

[108] Markus, Steele, and Steele 2000.

groups."[109] So the very notion of "integration" has become charged since it implies—or more exactly is taken to imply—that black Americans should aim to be white Americans.

This insistence on being recognized on one's own terms is itself one theme in a larger chorus: that the promise of racial equality made a generation ago has proven hollow; that the ideal of integration, of a color-blind society, is part of the weaponry of racial conservatives who wish to undermine the legitimacy of race-conscious policies like affirmative action; that black Americans should value what sets them apart as black Americans. These sentiments are not confined to narrow intellectual circles in black America. They can be found throughout the black community. So we have spent the chief part of our effort documenting the sense of distinctness that the largest number of black Americans feel by virtue of being black and the strains that many feel between themselves and white Americans. Both the sense of identity and the sense of strain are genuine. So, too, are the accomplishments, traditions, and the unique history of black Americans in America. But does it follow that, because black Americans have a strong sense of racial identity and feel a strong sense of solidarity with fellow black Americans, they do not adhere to the culture of America?

What Americans disagree about tends to capture the center of attention. What they agree on, to be taken for granted. But what Americans, black and white, agree on is of fundamental importance because it establishes the framework of politics itself. And we have been persuaded by our results that black Americans are as fully, as unconditionally, committed to American society and its core values as any other group of Americans.

We recognize that this claim of common ground will be received skeptically by many—including some who most wish it to be true. We only ask that you keep an open mind until we have had the chance to complete our presentation of the evidence. Up to this point, we have concentrated on showing that black Americans have a strong sense of pride in their identity as black Americans and a deep conviction about the wrongs that have been done—and continue to be done—to them as blacks in America. We mean to document in this chapter that they also have a bedrock commitment to

[109] Ibid., p. 239.

the core values of the American experience; that they have confidence in their ability to make a life for themselves and to succeed in America; and still more, that they are overwhelmingly committed to integration, to a society in which blacks and whites live together and work alongside one another and are judged by the same standards. It is not true that when it comes to core American values, black Americans line up on one side and white Americans on the other. The notion that if you know the color of an American's skin, you know also their sense of what is right, what is worthy of effort, what one owes to one's family, is long overdue for retirement. It is curiously hard for some to acknowledge that the operative word in "African American" is "American." That is our claim nonetheless.

Integration versus Racial Separatism

The thrusts of the black pride movement have been to accentuate the distinctiveness of blacks, celebrate points of difference between black and white Americans, and suggest that the divide between black Americans and white Americans not only cannot, but more insistently, should not, be erased. To go by the pronouncements of advocates of this movement, integration is no longer an ideal of African Americans. If it ever was an option, it is a path long since overgrown.

The public agenda, of course, is disproportionately shaped by those who write on and speak about public questions and attempt to influence directly the course of public action. And the views of those who are drawn to politics tend to be shaped partly by the fact that they are drawn to politics. As a result, the larger categories in which they view specific issues and the emphasis and interpretation they give to them tend to differ systematically from those of the public as a whole.

This disjuncture between the orientations of the politically prominent and those of citizens at large has nothing specifically to do with race. Purely as a matter of historical fact, it was research on the contrast between the belief systems of political elites and those of Americans taken as a whole that exposed the gap between the two.[110] But given that there tends, in greater or lesser degree, to be a disjuncture between the views of the politically prominent and ordinary citizens, it follows that if you want to know what black Americans in a community think, it is necessary to ask them, not those who claim to speak for them.

In this chapter we therefore propose to explore the attitudes of ordinary black Americans about integration and about racial separation. Is integration any longer an ideal for significant numbers of black Americans? To what extent has the idea of racial separation won their loyalty?

The notion of racial separatism can be used so loosely that it becomes a synonym for taking pride in a sense of distinctness as a black American. But it makes no sense to categorize Jewish (or Irish or Swedish or black) Americans as separatists for feeling a sense of distinctness and pride in being Jewish (or Irish or Swedish or black).

But, then, what is the right way to proceed? Our approach is this. Since there is no standardized method of defining racial separatism and integration, we will explore a whole variety of ways in which a sense of black separatism can express itself, and see whether they tell essentially the same story. The place to begin is, however, obvious—the ideal of integration. Following Brian Barry's classic definition, we take the heart of the ideal of integration to consist in "the belief that it is a desirable state of affairs for people who differ in certain given respects to mix socially and to share the same clubs, churches, political parties, housing areas, shops, schools, theatres, swimming pools, etc."[111] And since we wanted to go to the heart of the matter, the willingness and even desire to live side-by-side with one another, we asked our respondents whether they thought that:

> Blacks are better off living with other blacks in black neighborhoods rather than living with whites.

Look at the first bar of figure 4.1, and you will see that the reactions of our respondents are one-sided. More than 80 percent reject

---

[110] The literature on differences between the politically active and sophisticated and mass publics is enormous. For two classical studies, see McClosky, Hoffmann, and O'Hara 1960 and Converse 1964; for two more recent studies, see Zaller 1992 and Sniderman, Brody, and Tetlock 1991.

[111] Barry 1965, p. 122.

the idea that blacks are "better off living with other blacks in black neighborhoods rather than living with whites," and what is more, two out of every three who reject racial separatism do so strongly.[112]

Another indicator of the appeal of racial separatism is political loyalty—voting for black candidates because they are black. This second measure of racial separatism is less demanding than the first. And it is only natural to suppose that blacks in large numbers would endorse it. In fact, as the second bar of figure 4.1 shows, racial voting as an ideal is rejected overwhelmingly. Seventy-nine percent of our respondents reject the proposition that "blacks should always vote for black candidates when they run for an elected office," and more than two out of every three who reject this form of racial separatism do so strongly.[113] It is of course possible to object that requiring a readiness to *always* vote for black candidates puts the bar too high; that it should only be necessary to profess that you are willing to vote frequently or generally for black candidates. The price of accepting this objection, however, is watering down the notion of racial separatism, making it roughly synonymous with a readiness to say that you will give a black candidate the benefit of the doubt, other things equal. Racial separatism is only interesting, we mean to insist, if it represents a real readiness to separate.

Another indicator of separatist sentiments is giving primacy to considerations of race in the educational process. But it is necessary to put this idea in a way that goes beyond gesture and instead requires commitment. For example, for many years there has been a belief in the importance of having black teachers to provide black role models for black school children. We have no way to put an exact number on the proportion of people who share that belief. But it is certainly not confined to blacks, and in any case it is obvious that to believe black teachers can be role models for

---

[112] Fifty-five percent disagree strongly, and 29 percent disagree somewhat.

[113] In response to a quite differently worded item, Dawson reports that 50 percent of a 1993–94 national sample of blacks agree that blacks should form their own political party (Dawson 2001, p. 328). By contrast, in response to a question similarly worded to ours, Tate 1991 reports that only 19 percent of a 1984 national sample agree that blacks should always vote for black candidates when they run—a result virtually identical to ours—and that only 28 percent agree that blacks should form their own political party. On at least two items, Dawson's results represent sharp departures from previous studies and our own.

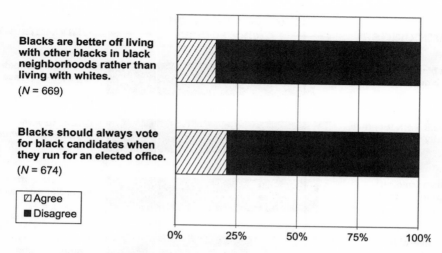

Figure 4.1. Racial Separatism

black children is not the same as advocating racial separatism. Simply put, because black Americans find value in being black does not mean that they think there is no value in living in a common society with white Americans. We therefore wanted to explore the reactions of blacks when considerations of race collide with considerations of merit. It is not, of course, that the two must necessarily collide. Often, perhaps most often, no choice between them needs to be made. But the issue of race can be difficult because sometimes the claims of race and merit—or competing conceptions of merit—must be weighed one against the other. Accordingly, we asked our respondents not whether black teachers can benefit black school children, but whether, in selecting teachers for black children, considerations of race should trump considerations of quality. Specifically we asked our respondents:

> Is it more important for schools in black neighborhoods to hire black teachers, or for these schools to select the most competent teachers regardless of race?

Given what we have already seen, it cannot be a surprise that the response was one-sided. In figure 4.2 we see that only a handful of our respondents believe that black schools should hire teachers who are black rather than hire the best teachers regardless of race. Our

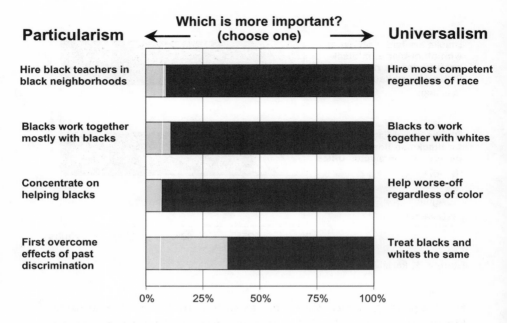

Which is more important?

Particularism ⟵⎯⎯ (choose one) ⎯⎯⟶ **Universalism**

Hire black teachers in black neighborhoods — Hire most competent regardless of race

Blacks work together mostly with blacks — Blacks to work together with whites

Concentrate on helping blacks — Help worse-off regardless of color

First overcome effects of past discrimination — Treat blacks and whites the same

0%   25%   50%   75%   100%

Figure 4.2. Racial Particularism

respondents virtually unanimously believe that the most competent candidate—regardless of race—should be hired.

Yet it sets the bar very high to ask that blacks agree that race should trump competence in order to classify them as racial separatists. So we would like to lower it a bit. Instead of asking whether blacks believe in racial separatism as a goal in itself, we ask whether they believe that it may be used as a means. Blacks, as we have seen, overwhelmingly reject the idea that blacks should live in black neighborhoods rather than living with whites. But because blacks may wish that blacks and whites ultimately live together as Americans, it does not follow that they think that the best way to achieve this is to commit themselves to integration right now. They may believe—and if much of the public rhetoric is right, in fact do believe—that the way for blacks to move forward is for blacks to work with other blacks, to advance the distinctive interests of blacks. On this view, it is necessary to achieve equality first in order to make integration possible later.

What do blacks think is the best course to make progress? We gave respondents the following choice:

To make real progress in achieving equality, is it more important for blacks to work together with whites, or to work together mostly with other blacks?

Notice that no ultimate values, whether of mutual understanding or of racial pride, are invoked. The question is put in strictly instrumental terms: what is the best way for blacks to achieve equality? And the answer, from the perspective of blacks, is clear-cut. As figure 4.2 shows, almost nine in every ten favor working together with white Americans; only about one in every ten favors working separately with other blacks. Integration again is endorsed virtually unanimously.

Or is it? Perhaps this is no more than political realism, a self-disciplined calculation that blacks must work together with whites because, given the imbalance of power between whites and blacks, blacks cannot make progress any other way. If so, support for working together across racial lines, although evidence of prudence, is not a proof of principle, of a judgment that setting aside racial lines is a good thing in and of itself.

Is it possible to tell the difference between the two, to determine whether this readiness to set race aside and work together with whites is based on a strictly instrumental calculation of political self-interest or a judgment about political principle? And supposing political calculations can be distinguished from political principles, what does it mean to set race aside—what, exactly, are the alternatives?

One alternative is straightforward. Blacks may favor a politics that is racially focused; that is, a politics specially focused on helping blacks. But what is the alternative to racial particularism? The temptation is to say, a politics that is color-blind. But to speak of blacks favoring a color-blind politics is to be bewitched by words. They may overwhelmingly reject racial separatism as an encompassing principle. They may one-sidedly believe that the right course to achieve equality—that is, both the most useful and the best-grounded strategy—is to work together with whites. Most importantly, they may adhere to principles of political judgment that in a defining sense are impartial. But that does not mean that they believe that the problems of blacks no longer call for special consideration. And it certainly does not mean that they want to dismantle affirmative action. What is at issue instead is a recognition that black and white Americans can both be badly-off—equally in need, equally deserving of assistance. To recognize this is not to believe that racial inequality has been overcome. Race is still tied up with being badly-off. But being badly-off, not being black, is the reason for assistance. This justification for assistance is a form of moral universalism, for it applies to those in need across-the-board, white or black.

To see the balance that blacks strike between a politics directed specially at their needs and one that is morally universalistic, we asked:

> Is it more important to help those who are worse-off regardless of their color, or to concentrate on helping blacks?

Notice that the second alternative addresses the issue of racial particularism directly. Our respondents thus have an unimpeded opportunity to favor a racially centered politics organized around assisting fellow blacks. Yet virtually without exception they reject this alternative. As figure 4.2 shows, more than nine in every ten believe instead that it is more important to help those who are worse-off "regardless of their color"; only a handful believe that it is more important to concentrate on helping blacks.

The black community includes many strains of opinion, some aggressively separatist. But our results document the representative position of the community as a whole, and our respondents consistently, and overwhelmingly, reject racial separatism in all of the assorted and various forms we have canvassed.

But a rejection of racial separatism is not the same thing as a commitment to a politics that transcends race. In order to assess this, we need to frame an alternative for a politics that is focused on blacks that carries with it an explicit and credible justification; and the best way to do this is to invoke the issue of racial injustice itself. So we asked:

> As things now stand, is it more important to treat blacks and whites the same, or to first overcome the effects of past discrimination?

It is a familiar theme of black public rhetoric that, until blacks and whites really are equal, it is necessary that they be treated differently. It is accordingly genuinely surprising that, even in the face of an explicit appeal to give priority to rectifying racial injustices, the largest number of our black respondents support the principle of equal treatment. Indeed, 64 percent of them believe that it is more important to treat blacks and whites the same, as the last bar of figure 4.2 shows. Of course a sizeable minority believe that it is more important first to overcome the effects of past discrimination. Moreover, because blacks are committed to common goals and common action does not mean that they believe that the position of blacks no longer is exceptional, that blacks no longer face racial discrimination, that there no longer is a need to take special, even unique, measures to address the problems that blacks uniquely suffer. It is, however, testimony to the power of the ideal of integration, of the appeal of a bond that transcends differences of race, that two out of every three of our respondents reject different standards for whites and blacks even as a temporary measure.

Counterstrains

If political separatism has a weak appeal, cultural separatism has a stronger charge, especially in the educational sphere. American education, it is true, seems always in the process of change, but one of the larger changes over the last generation has been the establishment, at both secondary and higher levels of education, of programs in black studies. These programs take an indefinite number of forms, making generalizations about them hazardous in the extreme. But a common premise is that blacks, by virtue of being black, have a distinctive identity, a distinct culture. And one reason that this cultural project has momentum is because the idea of a black culture resonates in the larger black community. It is all the more important, therefore, to explore how blacks understand the idea of a black culture.

One of the characteristics of American culture is its pluralism. An individual can belong to different subcultures while simultaneously belonging to the common American culture—for example, can see himself as Jewish and as American at the same time—if he or she wishes. The question is how blacks conceive of their cultural commitments. Does a commitment to a black culture preclude a commitment to a common culture? We accordingly asked:

> Is it more important to promote black culture as a separate culture, or to emphasize what Americans have in common?

For those who suppose that cultural separatism is the dominant chord in contemporary black thought, the responses are worth noting. As we see in figure 4.3, the overwhelming number of our respondents—about three in every four—reject the idea of promoting black culture as a separate culture, believing instead that it is more important to emphasize what Americans have in common.

Perhaps this is a result of the specific alternatives our respondents were asked to choose between; or, what is not quite the same thing, of the specific wording of either or both of the alternatives. So we posed another question with the same general alternatives of racial or cross-racial solidarity but in different language. Specifically, we asked:

> Is it more important to promote racial harmony between blacks and whites, or for blacks to fight for their rights, even if it means creating tension between blacks and whites?

Again the alternatives are between choosing in favor of common ground or racial solidarity. And again a solid majority—more than two in every three, as seen in figure 4.3—believe that "to promote racial harmony between blacks and whites" is more important than for "blacks to fight for their rights."

This result deserves comment on several fronts. First, it surely is true that the idea that whites should for once suffer some discomfort is not without appeal to a large number of blacks. But at least as assessed by the questions here, the number of blacks who have a consistent disposition to reject a common bond with whites is not similarly large: any reflexive readiness to favor opportunities to increase tensions between blacks and whites is conspicuous for its modesty.

We want to emphasize that although the proportion of blacks prepared to back racial solidarity if it comes at the expense of a greater division between blacks and whites fluctuates depending on how the issue of solidarity is defined, it always represents a substantial fraction of the black community; and even if it typically is

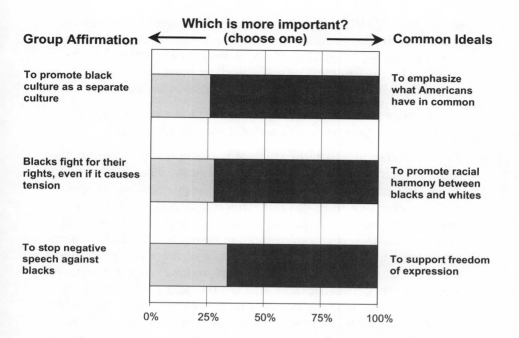

Figure 4.3. Racial Affirmation

a minority, it nonetheless represents a sizeable minority, usually about one-third. It is, even so, more difficult to elicit a response in favor of a greater division between blacks and whites than a cynical view would suggest. We ourselves supposed that, by framing this question in terms of a choice between harmony between blacks and whites and "blacks fighting for their rights," we had, if anything, stacked the deck in favor of a racially separatist response. Yet, less than a third of our respondents declared that it is more important for blacks to fight for their rights than "to promote racial harmony between blacks and whites."

Consider a final test. It is a well-established finding that ordinary citizens, though unanimously supporting the principle of free speech in the abstract, desert in droves when their attention is called to a conflicting concern—say, public safety.[114] This suggested

[114] The classic study is Stouffer 1992. See also McClosky and Brill 1983 and Sullivan, Piereson, and Marcus 1982.

to us the potential importance of undertaking a comparable—indeed, more demanding—test for black Americans. How would they choose, we wanted to know, if they had to choose between standing by the principle of free speech or preventing people from saying critical things about blacks? Accordingly we asked:

Is it more important to support freedom of expression, or to stop people from saying negative things about blacks?

For anyone familiar with the study of public opinion, the result may come as a surprise. An overwhelming majority of our black respondents—two in every three—stood behind the principle of free speech.

To be sure, one third did not. This is a minority, but not a tiny minority. In politics, minorities, if intense, can dominate majorities. And we have seen that a substantial minority in the black community wishes to promote black culture as a separate culture, support the idea that blacks should fight for their rights even if it means creating tension between blacks and whites, and rejects freedom of speech for those who say negative things about blacks. These ideas are of course only illustrative of an important strain of thought among black Americans, and though it is not the dominant strain, it nonetheless is worth trying to gauge its character. In particular, two questions are worth asking. First, to what extent do these various ideas about a separate black culture and the like constitute an integrated, internally coherent outlook or point of view in the black community? Second, to what extent are they fueled by, or at any rate associated with, the tide of racial identification that we have seen flowing in various degrees through the black community?

If these various ideas of racial strain and separation are part of a coherent outlook, then those who accept one of them should be more likely to accept the others. Indeed, the more true this is, the more tightly braided the set of ideas as a whole. Table 4.1 shows the extent to which acceptance of one of these ideas (shown in figures 4.1, 4.2, and 4.3) goes along with accepting the others. The outcome is obvious. One or two of the ideas are somewhat connected, but for the set of ideas as a whole, there is almost a complete absence of coherence or organization. (The average correlation is .07).

What, then, about the second question: whether these different expressions of strain and resistance to the larger American culture

TABLE 4.1
Correlations among Racial Strain and Separatism Items
(Correlation Coefficients)

	Vote Black	Live with Blacks	Black Teachers	Work with Blacks	Help Blacks	Overcome Past Discrimination	Black Culture	Fight for Rights
Vote Black	1.00							
Live with Blacks	.09*	1.00						
Black Teachers	-.02	.08*	1.00					
Work with Blacks	.20*	.04	.10*	1.00				
Help Blacks	.13*	-.01	.14*	.09*	1.00			
Overcome Past Discrimination	.12*	.07	-.02	.08	.08	1.00		
Black Culture	.02	.08	.25*	-.03	.12*	.13*	1.00	
Fight for Rights	.16*	.08	.13*	.13*	.12*	.13*	.09*	1.00
Stop Negative Speech	-.04	.08	.04	.09*	.00	-.08*	-.14*	.08

Note: Minimum $N = 607$; *$p < .05$.

TABLE 4.2
Correlations between Some Racial Strain Items and the Racial Identity
Measures
(Correlation Coefficients)

	Live with Blacks	Promote Black Culture	Stop Negative Speech
Autonomy	.25	.11	−.20
Afrocentrism	.15	.21	−.12
Common Fate	.13	.22	−.12
Build Pride	.17	.25	−.09

Note: Minimum N = 543; all $p < .05$.

are closely tied to the various forms of racial pride that we have
examined? In all, we have looked at nine indicators of racial strain
and separatism. Of the nine, we can find consistent relations with
our measures of racial ideology with only three of these indicators,
and as table 4.2 shows, they run in opposite directions. For two of
the indicators—whether blacks are better-off living with other blacks
and whether it is more important to promote a separate black culture or to emphasize what Americans have in common—taking
pride in being black encourages among black Americans an inclination to press for separation. For the other indicator—whether it is
more important to stop people from saying negative things about
blacks or to support freedom of speech—the direction of the rela-
tionships tends to be just the other way around: the more likely
blacks are to take pride in being black, the more likely they are to
support freedom of speech, not punishment of others who are critical of blacks. All in all, the conclusion to draw is that the various
expressions of racial separatism and strain do not form a coherent,
organized outlook in the larger black community, but that in a few
respects racial identification can reinforce a sense of separation.

Succeeding More, but Enjoying It Less: The "Alienation" of the Black Middle Class

The black middle class, we are told, is bitterly disappointed.
They were promised that the barriers to advancement would be

eliminated, that black Americans would have the same opportunities and be judged on the same terms as white Americans. They have
done their part. They have passed the educational hurdles; acquired
the skills; obtained the credentials; worked hard. Yet they haven't
achieved the success commensurate with their abilities and efforts.
White Americans may no longer parade their racism publicly, but it
is there all the same, expressed more subtly, stymieing black efforts
to get ahead. The result, to borrow the title of Ellis Cose's riveting
account, is "the rage of a privileged class."[115]

The anger, the sense of betrayal, of the black middle class has
become a popular theme. The most searching and comprehensive
analysis of it is Jennifer Hochschild's, *Facing Up To The American
Dream*.[116] Hochschild claims that a profound reversal has occurred in
the outlook of blacks. A generation ago, middle-class blacks were
more optimistic than poor blacks, less embittered about white
Americans, more confident that their lives would improve, more
committed to the American dream. But this has turned upside
down. Instead of being more optimistic and confident than poor
blacks, middle-class blacks now are more pessimistic, more embittered, less committed to the American dream. Hochschild presents
results gleaned from a large array of public opinion polls suggesting
that, by the 1980s and the 1990s, middle-class blacks had become
more likely than poor blacks to believe that whites want to keep
blacks down;[117] to doubt that blacks would have a fair chance to get
ahead;[118] to challenge whether blacks were making progress economically, even while acknowledging that they themselves were better-off financially;[119] to question whether African Americans can
reasonably anticipate achieving their dreams.[120]

It is a commonplace that someone who is badly-off and whose
circumstances in life are getting worse should be less confident
about his chances of success than a person who is comparatively
well-off and whose circumstances are getting better. It is accordingly

[115] Cose 1993.
[116] Hochschild (1995) provides a panoramic review of a wealth of studies of black
public opinion over the last half century. We have greatly profited from her exceptional study.
[117] See Hochschild 1995, table 4.1, p. 74.
[118] Ibid., table 4.2, pp. 76–77.
[119] Ibid., table 4.3, p. 79.
[120] Ibid., table 4.4, p. 81.

a paradox if blacks who are well-off, and who have become so over the last thirty years, should be less confident about their chances of success than blacks who are badly-off. And there is no question that the circumstances and prospects of middle-class blacks have dramatically improved over this period of time. As Hochschild herself observes, the proportion of blacks in the middle class increased from about one in every ten a generation ago to one in every three; the proportion of blacks with a college education increased by a factor of four; and the proportion of well-off blacks doubled between 1967 and 1992.[121] Middle-class blacks, all of the evidence suggests, are much better-off than they used to be, even if they still are not as well-off as well-off whites.[122] By contrast, the lot of poorer blacks has either stayed the same or gotten worse.[123] Yet according to Hochschild, middle-class blacks are less confident of success, less persuaded of the fairness of the American creed, even as they are making their way up the ladder. They are losing hope even as they are gaining ground. Just as they seemed to have the American dream within their grasp, it eluded them. They thought they had broken through, entered a world where they would be judged on their merits, not on the color of their skin. But prejudice did not disappear. The barriers to blacks did not disappear. They only became more subtle—and therefore all the more frustrating. So progress bred disappointment, anger, and estrangement. To quote Hochschild directly, "as the African American middle class has become larger, more powerful, and more stable, its members have grown disillusioned and even embittered about the American dream."[124] If true, this is a profoundly important—and a profoundly dispiriting— observation. It is profoundly important because both liberals and conservatives have always supposed that upward mobility is the ultimate solvent of racial inequality. It is profoundly dispiriting because, if the reality of getting ahead perversely winds up persuading blacks that they cannot really succeed, then what hope is there for ever transcending the American dilemma?

The question of whether black Americans, and particularly

---

[121] Ibid., pp. 43–45.

[122] Ibid., p. 44; a very important dimension of difference is accumulated wealth. For the best discussion of this basis for inequality, see Oliver and Shapiro 1995.

[123] Hochschild 1995. See also Jaynes and Williams 1989.

[124] Hochschild 1995, p. 72.

whether middle-class black Americans, have lost faith in the American dream is more difficult to answer than it may seem. Consider a typical question Hochschild uses: "Do you think in the next five [or ten] years, opportunities for blacks to get ahead will improve?"[125] She takes a negative answer to be evidence of being "disillusioned and even embittered about the American dream." But place yourself for a moment in the position of a middle-class black who is being interviewed in a public opinion survey and asked his or her views about matters of race. Here you are, taking part in a survey designed to represent the views of the country, being asked to register your views about the problem of race, presented with an opportunity to say what you think should be done. Surely you might take it that the question you actually are being asked is, "Do blacks now have things fine or does more need to be done to see that things become as they ideally should be?" And if you say that the opportunities for blacks to get ahead are getting better and better, doesn't this come down to saying that the problem of race essentially has been taken care of, and that all that is needed is time for things to work themselves out? And wouldn't you be even more likely to insist that much remains to be done if you were yourself comparatively well-off? We have after all seen that a sense of racial identification, and in particular a sense that what happens to other blacks makes a difference to what happens to you, is stronger precisely for middle-class blacks.

The question is not whether black Americans, middle-class or otherwise, believe that much still needs to be done to make racial equality a reality. They do. And Hochschild herself recognizes that the black middle class may be questioning whether opportunities for blacks to get ahead will improve, not necessarily because their confidence in the American dream has evaporated, but because they wish to show solidarity with blacks who are not doing as well. To tell whether middle-class black Americans have indeed lost confidence in the American dream, we need to explore not whether they believe that racial inequities persist—they do—but the rather different question of whether they believe they can make for themselves the sorts of lives one can and should enjoy in America.

---

[125] We are using as an example only one of the items that Hochschild cites, though the others could just as well be put in its place.

A Loss of Confidence?

To say that black Americans, and perhaps particularly middle-class black Americans, have lost confidence in the future can mean two quite different things. It may be a statement about external barriers to advancement that block black Americans' way forward. Or it may be a statement about internal impediments that limit their ability to make their way forward. The two, obviously, can be related. People will eventually lose confidence in their internal competence to succeed if the external barriers to their success are too high. But these two different senses in which a person can lose confidence are not the same. The first locates the problem in the world; the second locates it within the individual himself. The second is therefore disabling in a way that the first is not. It is possible to believe that you can overcome, or eradicate, external barriers to achievement provided you believe in your own capacity to achieve; it is not possible to have confidence in your chances of success, whether or not you believe you face external barriers, if you do not believe in your own capacity to achieve. The second possibility, the doubt about one's inner self rather than about the external world, is thus more ominous than the first. Just so far as it carries with it an undertone of personal defeat, it implies that middle-class blacks, even after experiencing success, believe that there really is no point in continuing to try to do still better. They don't have what it takes to get over the obstacles that face them.

How shall we tell if either, or both, are true? Consider the question of blacks' beliefs about their chances for success given that America is as it is. The issue, to repeat, is not whether black Americans believe that they face barriers to upward mobility, to doing better and being better-off. They do. The issue is whether, however high they believe those barriers are, they believe that they nonetheless can scale them. So rather than asking about the height of external barriers for blacks, and thus making race the issue, we instead ask about the future they see in store for themselves without mentioning race. Specifically we ask,

> Looking ahead five years from now, do you think your financial situation will be better than it is now, worse, or about the same as it is now?

If they say they think they will be worse-off, then this would be an indication that they lack confidence in the American promise of upward mobility, as the claim of an alienated black middle class suggests; if not, it would be a suggestion that the claims that the black middle class are giving up on the promise of the American experience are overdrawn.

A second indicator focusing on the internal, not the external, taps black Americans' self-perception of whether they have a sense of purpose and control in their lives. Just so far as they endorse sentiments like "nowadays a person has to live pretty much for today and let tomorrow take care of itself" and "you sometimes can't help wondering whether anything is worthwhile anymore," which are standard indicators of anomie, of feeling defenseless and helpless, they will show themselves to lack a sense of purpose and a feeling of control.[126]

Consider several possibilities. First, if the "alienation" of middle-class blacks involves a loss of confidence in the American promise of upward mobility, middle-class blacks will be more likely than working-class blacks to say that they will not be better-off in five years than they are now or, possibly, even that they will be worse-off. Second, if middle-class black "disillusion" involves a sense of personal defeat, middle-class blacks will be more likely to say that the world is meaningless, that the outcomes of events are arbitrary, that efforts to change or improve things are pointless. And third, if it involves both a loss of confidence in the world and in themselves, middle-class blacks will be both more pessimistic about their financial future and more susceptible to feelings of anomie.

To see which of these possibilities is closest to the truth of the matter, we compare middle-class and non-middle-class blacks with respect to their expectations of their financial future. As figure 4.4 shows, contrary to the general contention of a collapse of confidence and faith in the future, only a handful of our black respondents are pessimistic about their financial future, and the overwhelming majority—approximately three in every four—are optimistic that their financial situation will be better in five years than it is now. Education does make a difference, as Hochschild suggests, but in the opposite way that her theme of the collapse of middle-class black faith in the American dream suggests. It is the

[126] McClosky and Schaar 1965.

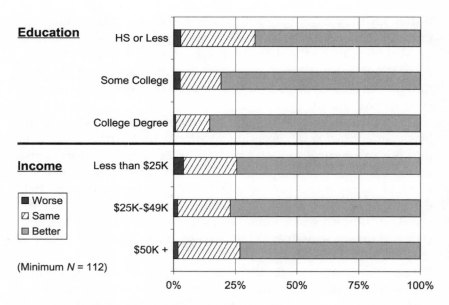

Figure 4.4. Financial Confidence—Five Years from Now

better-educated blacks who have the most confidence in their futures. Family income makes no difference.

And what about a faith that one's life is worthwhile, meaningful, that one can have confidence in the future and not simply have to live from day to day, without any sense of what tomorrow will bring? As previously mentioned, our measure of anomie attempts to isolate the diffuse concern, asking whether respondents agree or not with the following statements:

> You sometimes can't help wondering whether anything is worthwhile anymore; and Nowadays a person has to live pretty much for today and let tomorrow take care of itself.

The higher people's score on this measure, the less their faith that life is meaningful, subject to their control, responsive to their effort. If middle-class blacks have lost confidence in the future (whether class is measured by education or income), then they will be more likely to score high on anomie than working-class blacks. In fact, it is just the other way around. Middle-class blacks are more likely to believe that life is meaningful, the future pre-

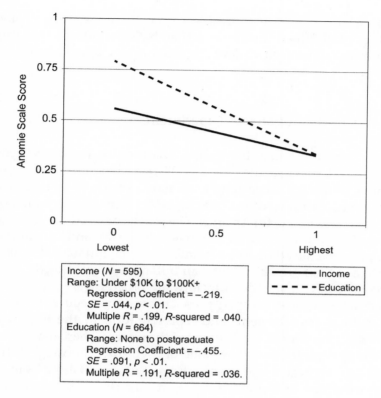

Figure 4.5. Anomie by Income and Education

dictable. Thus the better educated are black respondents, the lower their scores on anomie, not the higher (see the dotted line in figure 4.5). Similarly, the higher the income of our black respondents, the lower their scores on anomie, not the higher (see the solid line in figure 4.5).

This, surely, is what we should have expected to see. Who seriously doubts that people who are better-off, white or black, are more likely to find the world to be comprehensible than those who are badly-off, poorly educated, pushed to the margins of the larger society? Who would argue that those who are worst-off should be more confident about their financial future than those who are best-off? But because our black respondents believe that *they* can do well in America, it does not follow that they believe that *blacks as a whole* can do the same. Our object now, therefore, is to explore whether black Americans, even if they have confidence that they themselves can succeed, believe that black Americans as a group can succeed.

The "Life Chances" Experiment

Some prominent blacks have charged that there has been a new betrayal. America, they say, has allowed a parade of newcomers to enter. Although some new immigrants continue to be drawn from the historical reservoir of Europe, the principal currents now flow from Asia and Latin America. These newcomers differ in a host of ways from one another: in nationality, language, and race, in class of origin and education, in economic resources and market skills at the time of their arrival. Yet after an initial period of struggle, these newcomers have made their way forward, progressively enjoying an increasing measure of prosperity, social acceptance, educational and professional advancement, and representation in the dominant political and economic institutions of the society. These newcomers came only recently, and they came of their own choosing. If they have been mistreated and been victims of discrimination, as many have, they have not suffered anything like the exploitation and discrimination that blacks have endured. Yet, in the view of some blacks, these newcomers have gotten ahead of blacks. And not only have they done better than blacks, but they have made their way past blacks partly by taking advantage of social policies brought into being by the struggle and sacrifices of blacks.

Because some black activists make this charge does not mean that the black public views things the same way. But it certainly is possible that the black public believes that newcomers are passing them by. And that is why we designed and carried out the "Life Chances" experiment.

The aim of the experiment is to find out how blacks rate their prospects in comparison with those of other groups. One angle of the comparison to be made is obvious: how blacks rate their chances of success compared to those of the fastest growing minority in America—Mexican Americans. But a general benchmark is just as important. For it certainly is possible that blacks may have a systematically different opinion of the chances of minorities—black or brown—enjoying a good life in America than those of Americans generally. Accordingly, in the Life Chances experiment respondents are assigned randomly to one of three experimental conditions. In the first condition, in order to see how black Americans rate the chances of people in general to have a good life, they are asked whether they agree or disagree that:

> If people work hard enough, they can make a good life for themselves.

In the second, in order to see how they rate the chances of a "newcomer" minority, they are asked whether they agree that:

> If Mexican Americans work hard enough, they can make a good life for themselves.

And in the third condition, in order to see how they rate their own chances, they are asked:

> If black Americans work hard enough, they can make a good life for themselves.

Notice that rather than impose on them a narrow or arbitrary conception of what is a good life, we ask whether a group "can make a good life for themselves," leaving our respondents free to define the character of a good life as they believe appropriate. Notice also that, in asking whether people are in a position to make a good life for themselves, we have added the condition that "they work hard enough." A stipulation that people must do their part to make their life go well does not seem inappropriate. The question is not whether success is assured merely because it is desired, guaranteed regardless of whether one makes an effort to achieve it or not. The question instead is whether, given a readiness on their part to try, African Americans believe that they can make a good life for themselves in America.

There are two prongs of comparison in the Life Chances experiment. One is how our black respondents rate their chances relative to people in general. As the first column of figure 4.6 shows, approximately nine in every ten agree (either strongly or somewhat) that if people work hard they can make a good life for themselves. Black Americans are thus overwhelmingly in agreement that people in

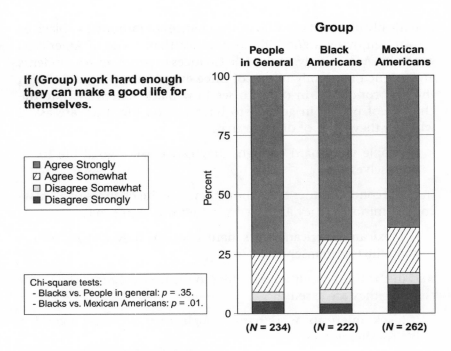

Figure 4.6. Chances for a Good Life

general can fashion a good life for themselves in America. The question is, how do they rate the prospects of black Americans to make a good life for themselves, as compared to the chances of people in general?

If you compare the first and second columns in figure 4.6, you will see that blacks rate their chances just as highly as they do the chances of others in general. Contrary to suggestions of blacks being enveloped by a sense of helplessness or hopelessness, they are as confident about the ability of blacks to create and enjoy a worthwhile life as that of people in the society as a whole. And just so far as making a good life is of fundamental importance, the results of the Life Chances experiment are worth highlighting.

But what about the second prong of the comparison? Do blacks look at other minorities resentfully? Do they believe that those other groups have gone past blacks and now have a better chance at a good life in America than blacks themselves?

It surely is not difficult to imagine that black Americans regard other minorities with a mixture of emotions, including resentment. The others, after all, are newer to America and, for all of the obstacles they have had to face, they have never been weighed down by the unique burden of discrimination and exploitation under which blacks have had to labor. Yet, these new minorities benefit from programs originally established to assist blacks, and to all appearances they are steadily making their way up the ladder in American society, perhaps even leaving blacks behind.

If blacks do indeed feel that they have been left behind, then they should rate the chances of Mexican Americans to make a good life for themselves to be better than those of blacks. Compare, then, the judgments of our black respondents for the life chances of blacks and Mexican Americans. Looking at the second and third columns of figure 4.6, the first thing we see is the similarity in the optimism for both. Then, looking more closely, you will see that, instead of blacks being more likely to believe that Mexican Americans have a better future than they, to the extent that they see any difference at all, it is just the other way around: blacks believe that *their own* prospects are better than those of Mexican Americans. The difference is small, but statistically significant. In short, there is no evidence to suggest that blacks are envious of the success of others. It would be a mistake to minimize the significance of this result.

There is another way to read the results of the Life Chances experiment. Is it possible that our respondents are not offering a descriptive judgment—a judgment, that is, about the way they believe the world to be as a matter of fact—but instead a prescriptive one, a judgment about the way they believe the world ought to be? On this interpretation, hearing the introductory phrase, "If black Americans (or Mexican Americans, the particular group makes no difference) work hard enough . . . " triggers a normative affirmation of the work ethic rather than a descriptive evaluation of life chances. So interpreted, respondents don't want to be put in the position of appearing to lack faith in the work ethic, and so they respond that yes, black Americans or Mexican Americans can indeed make a good life for themselves, even if as an empirical matter they believe that either or both will *not* succeed whether they work hard or not. But this is a counterargument that undercuts itself. For it amounts to saying that African Americans are so attached to the American ideal of opportunity and self-reliance that they respond as they do because they know that, as good Americans, this is what they ought to say, even if they don't believe it. And if they are indeed so attached to the norms of the American experience, it is not clear in what sense they can be said to have given up on them.

Multiculturalism or Commonality of Values?

"We are all," Nathan Glazer contends, "multiculturalists now," our undeniable continuing disagreements over the pinwheel term "multiculturalism" being not about the principle, but merely about its interpretation and application.[127] It is, in fact, not altogether obvious who "we" are. But Glazer's words have a ring of truth. On many ceremonial occasions, pride of place now goes not to the idea of liberty, nor to the rights of citizens under the Constitution, nor to individualism in its various chords, but rather to diversity as a value.

Contemporary American culture, viewed from the perspective of multiculturalism, has no legitimate common core. It is more nearly an aggregation of distinctive, autonomous, coherent cultures corresponding to distinct social, ethnic, and racial groups. Public institutions, on this view, have a duty to recognize, preserve, and respect the practices and perspectives of manifold cultures—among them Native American culture, Hispanic culture, Asian culture, and of course, African American culture.

The case for multiculturalism is not meant to rest on the specific merits of the outlook and history of any particular group. But although the argument for multiculturalism is made in universalistic terms, what has given it a hold on the American conscience is not the parade of groups it includes. It is the fact that so many black Americans remain so badly-off. For all that has been done, by way of both public and private action, and for all the progress that has been made, the problems that remain are daunting. Rates of illegitimacy are high, as are those of single-parent households; incarceration of black males; infant mortality and morbidity; homicide as a cause of death for young adults; and school dropouts, particularly in the inner cities.[128] In some circles, there is a readiness to back proposals

---

[127] Glazer 1997.
[128] Jaynes and Williams 1989.

that would have been unthinkable a generation ago—high schools specially restricted (or shall we say "officially segregated") to black males, for example. And specific proposals to one side, there is a broad desire to acknowledge and honor the accomplishments and unique experiences of black Americans. This desire has a number of sources, but in the words of Cornell West, it is rooted most deeply in a spreading concern about "the profound sense of psychological depression, personal worthlessness, and social despair so widespread in black America."[129]

Hence the politics of memory, culture, identity. Through a connection with their history and culture, it is suggested, blacks can repair a loss of values, religious and moral, and prevent a collapse into nihilism. But for culture to ground a distinctive racial identity, it is necessary for blacks to appreciate that there are indeed two cultures—one white, one black. To be sure, black culture has been intertwined with the American experience. But it is independent of it and reaches back far before it. It is separate, distinct, and for many purposes, self-sufficient.

We recognize that an emphasis on a separate black culture can spring from a desire to honor the distinctive history and accomplishments of black Americans. We recognize, too, that blacks have shared a distinctive historical experience and have, in consequence, a sense of a distinct identity, not to mention distinctive views on a range of subjects, very much including politics. But this sense of distinctiveness, we have become persuaded, has obscured the extent to which black and white Americans share a common set of values.

Consider two of the core values of the national culture—law and order, on the one side, and individual freedom on the other. Each is a foundational value, and each inevitably collides on occasion with the other. Accordingly, in the course of our interviews, we began a series of questions about political and social values by remarking that:

> Here are some values that everyone agrees are important. But sometimes we have to choose one value over another. If you absolutely had to choose between each of the following two values, which is the more important?

[129] West 1993, pp. 12–13.

Then, as one part of this series of questions, we asked:

How about guaranteeing law and order in society, or guaranteeing individual freedom? If you had to choose between these two, which would you say is more important?

Then, after they have chosen between them, we went on to ask:

Would you say that [guaranteeing law and order, or individual freedom, depending on which of the two they had picked] is much more important, somewhat more important, or only a little more important?

Every person can thus be distinguished depending on which value, law and order or individual freedom, he or she chooses as the more important, and in addition, how much more important than the other he or she judged it to be. Their answers have been scored to run from 0 to 1: the lower the score, the more important people think that law and order is, relative to individual freedom; the higher the score, the more important they think that individual freedom is, compared with law and order. For purposes of comparison, we compare the responses of our Chicago sample to a random sample of the country as a whole.[130] And since no group, black or white, is a monolith, we also consider points of similarity and difference between generations and educational strata both within and between black and white Americans.

Table 4.3 summarizes the choices of black and white Americans asked to choose between freedom and order. A score of more than .5 signals an overall preference for freedom, of less than .5 for order. Recognizing that both blacks and whites fall on both sides, one can see that, forced to choose between the two, black Americans choose law and order over individual freedom. This result, one might gratuitously observe, fits a common impression that black Americans are specially drawn to law and order appeals because they are specially exposed to the violence and chaos of life in the inner cities. It

[130] We draw here on the 1998–99 Multi-Investigator Study, funded by the National Science Foundation. This survey was carried out from June 21, 1998, through March 7, 1999, on a nationwide random-digit telephone sample by the Survey Research Center at the University of California, Berkeley. The target population for the study is all English-speaking adults, 18 years of age or older, residing in households with telephones, within the 48 contiguous states. There were 1,067 completed cases, with a response rate of 55.8 percent.

TABLE 4.3
Individual Freedom versus Law and Order by Age and Education
(Means between 0 and 1; High Score Means Individual Freedom)

A. Blacks (Chicago)

	Education		
	High School or Less	Some College	College Graduate
Age			
18–30	.47	.47	.21
31–50	.35	.34	.28
51+	.24	.36	.29
TOTAL	.35	.39	.27

Note: $N = 622$; minimum cell $N = 15$; overall mean = .35.
ANOVA test: Age $p < .01$; Education $p = .03$; Interaction $p = .09$.

B. Whites (National)

	Education		
	High School or Less	Some College	College Graduate
Age			
18–30	.41	.47	.49
31–50	.34	.42	.45
51+	.35	.34	.44
TOTAL	.36	.41	.45

Note: $N = 818$; minimum cell $N = 39$; overall mean = .40.
ANOVA test: Age $p = .07$; Education $p = .01$; Interaction $p = .68$.
Source: 1998–99 Multi-Investigator Survey.

is all the more revealing, therefore, to observe the reactions of white Americans. They also favor law and order over individual freedom, and they do so, what is more, by a similar margin (the average score for blacks being .35, for whites .40).

The similarity is striking. But the question of whether (and in what sense) there are distinct cultures is complex. The beliefs and preferences of two groups may be similar in the aggregate, but the patterns of commitment within them may differ. As table 4.3 shows, it is perfectly true that the "average" response of blacks and of whites is very nearly interchangeable. But it also is true, as you can see by looking along the columns, that there is a marked difference between blacks and whites depending on their level of education. Among whites, the least educated are the most likely to favor law and order; the most educated, the most likely (comparatively) to favor individual freedom. Among blacks, very nearly the opposite is closer to the mark. If one looks closely at table 4.3, it can be seen that the reason for this lies in the interplay of education and age. It is younger and middle-aged well-educated blacks who are more concerned about the need to establish law and order as against their similarly well-educated white counterparts, who are comparatively more committed to the value of individual freedom. But these differences of detail noted, it is the overall similarity of the views of whites and blacks that is striking.

Consider, then, the tension between the values of science and religion. A variety of ways are at hand to evade a collision between the two, but for many people it is hard to carry out the projects of a well-rounded life, and perhaps especially those of forming a family and raising children, without at some point facing a conflict between these two outlooks on life. For they represent not merely different ways of making sense of the experiences of life, but, in some circumstances at least, different ways of assigning them value. This particular clash of values—between the claims of religion and those of science—is worth looking at for another reason. A standard (one is tempted to say, stereotypical) feature of the portrait of black Americans is a distinctive commitment on their part to religion. Just so far as this is so, black Americans should be more likely than whites to believe that religion takes priority over science. To see if this is indeed so, we asked that if they had to choose between the two options below, which would be more important:

Encouraging belief in God, or a modern scientific outlook.

And then, whichever they said was the more important, we asked how much more important. Again their answers were scaled from 0 to 1: the larger the number, the more importance attached to science; the smaller the number, the more the importance attached to religion.

Looking first at the responses of blacks, you can see that their choice is one-sided. They overwhelmingly choose in favor of

TABLE 4.4
Scientific Outlook versus Belief in God by Age and Education
(Means between 0 and 1; High score means Scientific Outlook)

A. Blacks (Chicago)

	Education		
	High School or Less	Some College	College Graduate
Age			
18–30	.11	.10	.06
31–50	.05	.05	.05
51+	.08	.08	.06
TOTAL	.08	.08	.05

Note: N = 643; minimum cell N = 16; overall mean = .07.
ANOVA test: Age p = .03; Education p = .76; Interaction p = .92.

B. Whites (National)

	Education		
	High School or Less	Some College	College Graduate
Age			
18–30	.22	.29	.50
31–50	.14	.21	.28
51+	.09	.17	.27
TOTAL	.13	.22	.31

Note: N = 809; minimum cell N = 36; overall mean = .20.
ANOVA test: Age p < .01; Education p < .01; Interaction p = .37.
Source: 1998–99 Multi-Investigator Survey.

encouraging a belief in God (table 4.4). Moreover, if you look at their responses as a function of age and education, you will see that this one-sided commitment cuts clean across generational and educational differences. Indeed, there is no statistically significant difference between the responses of the least educated blacks and those of the most educated. And the effect of age, although statistically significant, is small and is not in a consistent direction. This is consistent with the picture of religiosity as especially central to the lives of black Americans from all backgrounds.

Look now at the reactions of whites. They, too, overwhelmingly choose in favor of encouraging a belief in God as more important than a modern, scientific outlook. Whites, it is true, are not quite so uniform in their avowal of religion: their average score is .20, compared to an average score of .07 for blacks. Moreover, the pattern of generational and educational differences among whites themselves is suggestive of an emerging difference. Younger whites and whites who are well-educated, though still in the largest number choosing religion over science, are significantly more sympathetic to the importance of a scientific outlook, suggesting that the gap between the outlook of blacks and of whites may widen in the future. But having spotlighted this point of dissimilarity, what stands out is the degree to which both blacks and whites favor a religious outlook over a scientific one.

We are certainly not arguing that blacks and whites have an identical view of the layers of the American historical experience. Blacks have had to bear a unique burden of suffering, and they have formed a unique body of historical memories in order to memorialize and respond to this legacy of suffering. But it is essential to get the proportions of distinctness and commonality right, and viewing the American experience through the new prism of multiculturalism invites distortion. It encourages the observer to blow up the differences between groups and minimize the differences within them. The effect is to see black and white Americans (and a gallery of others, too) as each embodying a way of life: separate, independent, committed to competing ideals, competing traditions. The results from our study—and indeed from the others of which we are aware[131]—could not be more at odds with the new stereotyping of ethnic and racial groups.

---

[131] Referring to his own earlier work (1976), Triandis (1988) takes the position that "overall, the similarities of black and white subjective cultures are much more overwhelming than the differences" (p. 36). He adds by way of both qualification and reaffirmation that "although with respect to black culture the extreme assimilationist position is usually not taken, the implication that blacks who are psychologically white are 'good' can be found in many of these editorials. In fact, the Triandis (1976) data indicate that the black middle class is already psychologically white. The cultural differences in subjective culture are observed only in the case of blacks who live in ghettoes" (p. 41).

A Crucible Test of Common Values—
The SAT Experiment

The evidence underscores the ground of values common to black and white Americans. Yet why should we believe that it is possible in a public opinion interview to gauge what people truly do value? What does it take to say that you believe, for example, in the value of achievement and the importance of hard work when you are being interviewed over the phone? There are no consequences to face, no necessity subsequently to act in a way consistent with the principles you have just professed. You have spoken to a stranger, under a seal of anonymity. It cost you nothing to say that you believe in the value of achievement.

It is no wonder that skepticism abounds about whether what people say in a public opinion interview has much to do with how they act outside of it. And if there is skepticism in general, it is far deeper when it comes to matters of race. Most often, skepticism is directed at white Americans' professions of good will to blacks. But an undercurrent of cynicism also bubbles up when it comes to blacks' professions of commitment to a value like that of achievement. Black Americans may say that they think that the person who has worked the hardest and done the best should get the promotion at work or win a place in law school. But what about when the issue is not espousing the value of achievement in the abstract, but of standing behind it when it comes at the expense of black Americans? How will blacks respond then? Will they stick with the value of achievement? Or will they choose, if choose they must, to protect and promote the needs and interests of fellow blacks?

Politically, the most dramatic clash between considerations of race and the claims of achievement has occurred between the requirements of affirmative action in college admission decisions and the use of standardized tests of academic aptitude and achievement. If admissions were to be made purely on standardized test results and academic records, the proportions of blacks admitted to first-tier universities would be radically slashed.[132] Partly to avoid confining the issue to matters of race, it has been argued that con-

---

[132] Bowen and Bok 1988.

siderations of class should underpin affirmative action. If it is inequality that justifies affirmative action, and not the exploitation of blacks uniquely, then the crucial consideration should be whether a person has less than others, not whether he is black regardless of whether he has less than others or not. Moreover, it is uncontested that the scores that students earn on standardized tests of aptitude or achievement may reflect the social circumstances in which they grew up. Two individuals indistinguishable in their native abilities can score quite differently on their college SATs because one had the advantage of growing up in favorable circumstances, with a father and mother who valued education and had the means to see that he or she benefited from the best of schooling, and the other did not. It is therefore possible, and indeed in some circles popular, to advocate class-based affirmative action with an eye to taking the issue of race out of the issue of affirmative action.

Considerations of class should not be collapsed into considerations of race, and vice versa. Yet there manifestly *is* a connection between the two. Blacks remain disproportionately likely to belong to households falling below the poverty line, to be raised in homes headed by a single parent, to grow up in places where life is nasty and short. Blacks thus suffer all too often the double burden of race and poverty, and however things look from the perspective of white Americans, for blacks the connection between racial inequity and economic and social disadvantage is plain to see.

Moreover, the collision between considerations of racial equity and the value of achievement need not be direct or head-on. In backing extra measures on behalf of fellow blacks to enlarge, for example, their horizon of opportunity at colleges and professional schools, blacks need not take the position that they are rejecting individual merit as the standard for success. It is perfectly possible to believe that when a choice must be made between applicants to college, whoever is best qualified—black or white—should be chosen and also to believe that standardized tests, as they presently are composed and administered, are biased against blacks and therefore should be discounted. It also is possible to believe that, given the obstacles that blacks uniquely confront, they must be better and work harder just to score as well as whites on standardized tests. And in any event, a commitment to merit, certainly as it is captured in the form of standardized achievement tests, is not an all-or-nothing proposition. Talent takes many forms, and standardized test scores surely cannot capture the full band of individual imagination, orig- inality, and intelligence.

All of these considerations represent an arsenal of principled arguments that can be mobilized against relying on standardized test scores as the single or necessarily decisive consideration for the college admission of minorities, and it forms the backdrop of the "Standardized Aptitude Test (SAT)" Experiment. The objective in designing the SAT experiment was to see whether—at the margins— blacks would prefer to admit more blacks into colleges than always to select the student with the higher score; the objective was not to see if blacks reject standardized tests out of hand or would choose to admit blacks in preference to whites no matter how large the differ- ence in their academic accomplishments. It is only that differences on standardized tests sometimes are small and should not be allowed to obscure larger considerations of providing justice and enlarging opportunity. The primary aim of the SAT experiment therefore is to see at what point blacks consider a difference in scores between white and black applicants to be small enough so that it should not, by itself, rule out a fellow black.

The experiment begins with a description of two young men who are applying to college: George, who is black, and Sam, who is white. They both took the same "college entrance exam." Sam scored 80 out of a possible 100 points—a high enough score to establish him as a good candidate, but not so high for him auto- matically to be admitted. Sam's score always is the same. But since the aim is to see at what point a difference between two people's scores is too small to count, George's score is varied, by increments of 5, from a low of 55 to a high of 75.[133] The result is a whole span of differences: at the largest, the white candidate does overwhelm- ingly better than the black, outscoring him by 25 points; at the smallest, the white candidate does barely better than the black, outscoring him by only 5 points. And since we have three scores in between, we are well placed to tell at what point blacks judge that the difference between the scores of black and white candidates is no longer large enough to be decisive in and of itself.

---

[133] George always scores lower than Sam because the issue of affirmative action otherwise would not arise. George's possible scores are: 55, 60, 65, 70, 75.

In order to get at the role of social class as a consideration for affirmative action, we systematically varied the social backgrounds of the two candidates in the experiment. It is important to consider all of the possibilities. Blacks may feel that overcoming the disadvantages of being poorly-off is an important consideration in its own right. Alternatively, they may feel that class becomes a relevant consideration only when it is coupled with race. To gauge all the possibilities, one half of the time George's father is a doctor; the other half, the father is out of work. The same is done for Sam's father. One half of the time he is a doctor, the other half of the time, he too, is out of work. There are thus four scenarios in all: two when a white and black applicant have the same social starting point (whether high or low); one when a black has had the advantage over a white; and of course crucially, one when a black candidate from a disadvantaged background must compete with a white candidate from a middle- or upper–middle class background. After the two young men are described, we then ask:

> If the college can only accept one of the two young men, who do you think should be admitted—George, because of the obstacles faced by blacks, or Sam, because his score on the entrance exam was higher?

Notice how directly the dilemma is posed. On the one side, every one is reminded that the score of the white applicant on the entrance exam was higher, even if it very often is only slightly higher. On the other side, the case for admitting the black applicant because of the continuing burden of discrimination and disadvantage that blacks bear is driven home directly, unambiguously, without a possibility of misunderstanding.

The heart of the matter is the readiness of blacks to favor a fellow black. Our intuition, to be altogether clear, was that when the difference between the two in their entrance examinations was small, blacks would disregard the scores. Indeed, since this seemed a sure bet, the real point of the design of the experiment was to determine at what point blacks perceive a difference in scores between a black and a white applicant to be small enough to favor a fellow black. Was it only the smallest possible difference, 5 points? Or was a difference of 10 points, from the perspective of a black deciding on the chances of a fellow black, too small to be decisive? Or perhaps a difference of 15 points could be set aside, in the interests of racial justice?

In setting up the SAT experiment, we certainly expected that at some point the difference between the scores of the black and of the white candidate would be so small as to be brushed aside. We were pretty sure that most other people, asked to make a prediction, would predict the same thing. But we wanted to get a more definite grip on the problem, to get a basis for a more specific set of expectations. So we took advantage of a session at the Summer Institute for Political Psychology, run jointly by the departments of psychology and political science at Ohio State University. The Institute enrolls graduate students interested in the field of political psychology for a month of intensive training. The students are selected from across the country, and include a smattering of postdoctoral students from abroad. During one session, the design of the SAT experiment was explained in detail, accompanied by an account, in very general terms, of our expectations. Then a question was posed to all participants. When is a difference in scores between the black candidate, George, and the white candidate, Sam, small enough so that it will be discounted by a majority of black respondents?

The Institute psychologists agreed, without debate, that when the gap in scores was very large, that black respondents overwhelmingly would decide that the candidate with the higher score should be admitted, even though the higher scoring candidate is white. The interesting question, it seemed to them as to us, is at what point the difference in scores would not be the decisive consideration. Table 4.7 summarizes their predictions.

As you can see, our panel of judges agreed unanimously that when the gap in scores is very wide—either 20 or 25 points—black respondents would choose Sam, the white candidate, in preference to George, the black one. And they also agreed unanimously that when the gap in scores is narrower, a majority of blacks would choose the black candidate to be admitted to college rather than the white, even though the white scored higher on the admission test. Still more interesting, a majority of the judges believed that the gap in scores does not have to be small in absolute terms in order to be brushed aside as too small to be decisive. Just over two out of every three of the judges predicted that a majority of black respondents would chose the black candidate over the white one, even if the

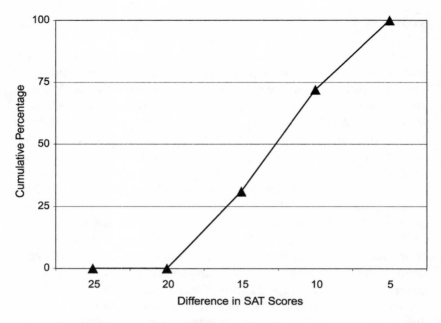

(N = 29 political psychology graduate students)

Figure 4.7. Judges Predicting Racial Favoritism

black candidate scored lower on the admission test by 10 points compared to the white applicant. It is also worth observing that every person venturing a prediction at the Institute for Political Psychology predicted that the difference in scores would at some point be small enough that it would be considered by a majority of blacks as too small to be the decisive factor in choosing which of the two candidates should be admitted to college.

Now, having made this effort to define what we should see, what is it that we actually see? Which person, George, the black candidate, or Sam, the white one, do black respondents believe should be picked, if a choice has to be made between the two? At what point is a difference in their test scores small enough so that a majority of black respondents believe that it is too small to be decisive?

Figure 4.8 shows the likelihood that the candidate with the higher score, that is the white candidate, will be chosen as a function of the size of the difference between the scores of the white and

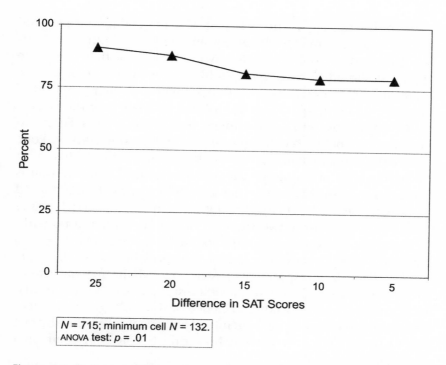

N = 715; minimum cell N = 132.
ANOVA test: p = .01

Figure 4.8. College Admissions by SAT Scores: Percent Favoring Admission of White Applicant

the black candidate. Our panel of judges—not to mention the two of us—were sure the proportion of blacks choosing the white applicant would plummet as the difference in SAT scores became progressively smaller, and fairly quickly. But what we actually see is not at all what we expected to see. Blacks overwhelming choose the candidate who scored higher, even though the higher-scoring candidate always is white, and they choose the white candidate over the black however small the difference between their scores.[134]

It is true, and we do not wish to neglect this, that the margin preferring the white candidate does drop as the gap between the test scores of the two applicants shrinks. But it is essential to see clearly, unequivocally, the meaning of this decline. Look at the choices that our black respondents make where the difference between the

[134] In figure 4.8, we ignore the randomly assigned occupations of the two fathers. We thus average over any occupation effects.

scores of the two applicants is largest. Where the difference is a full 25 points, approximately 90 percent felt the white should be admitted. Now look at the proportion who also decide that the white applicant should be preferred to a black one where the difference between them is a mere five points. Approximately eighty percent of black respondents still choose the white candidate over the black.

The finding of the SAT experiment thus comes to this. Forced to make a choice between two applicants for college, one black and one white, blacks overwhelming believe that the one who did better on the admission test should be the one that is admitted. And that is true even though this means that a white student will be admitted at the expense of a black. And what is more, it is true even where the difference between the two students' scores is small, and notwithstanding the fact that an appeal is explicitly made to blacks to side with the black student "because of the special obstacles faced by blacks." Our black respondents instead overwhelmingly adhere to the rule that the student with the best test scores should get priority. We think that this is striking evidence of the willingness of blacks not simply to endorse the principle of achievement in the abstract but to stand by it, even when honoring it comes at their own expense.

What about class and affirmative action? Viewed outside of the context of race, the positions of the black and of the white candidates may look the same. But it is not obvious that the position of the two is the same. A middle-class white, one may argue, is likely to have had a (comparatively) easy time in making his way forward. The middle-class black still had to overcome special obstacles by virtue of being black. Table 4.5 shows the judgments of who should be admitted, taking into account the status of their families. Two things stand out. First, it makes no difference to blacks if the black candidate's father is a doctor or out of work. Second, it does make a difference if the white candidate's is well-off or not. Blacks are more likely to favor a black candidate in preference to a white one when the white candidate comes from an advantaged background. Nevertheless, our major finding is that blacks place measures of achievement ahead of considerations of race.

It is surely striking that our black respondents overwhelmingly pick the white student over a fellow black even when the difference in their admission scores is very small. And it is not difficult to see

TABLE 4.5
Effect of Father's Status on College Admission Choice
(Percent Favoring Admission of *White* Applicant)

	Father of White Applicant	
	Doctor	*Out of Work*
Father of Black Applicant		
Doctor	77	90
Out of Work	78	87

Note: N = 715; minimum cell N = 166.
ANOVA test:
–Father of White Applicant: $p < .01$.
–Father of Black Applicant: $p = .71$.
–Interaction: $p = .54$.

how this result could be put to polemical use in discussions over affirmative action. We have therefore tried to be critics of our own result. Both working on our own and consulting with colleagues, the strongest objection we could identify is this. Achievement is a value in the larger culture. When blacks are being interviewed by a representative of that larger culture, they want to say the right thing. So can it be surprising, this line of reasoning runs, that when they are interviewed by a white, they say that the applicant with the high score, who is white, should be admitted. Indeed, the fact that they do so even when the difference between the scores of the white and of the black students is very small is a tip-off that they are only saying what they think they should say rather than what they really think.

Call this the "masking" objection.[135] The underlying intuition is that blacks adopt a mask when they are with members of the larger culture and act as if the values of that culture are theirs: but when they are with members of their own culture, they remove the mask, and express their true values. Suppose that the "masking objection"

[135] We want to express our gratitude to Darren Davis, who is a leading researcher on race-of-interviewer effects, among other things, and who helped guide us through the relevant research. See Anderson, Silver, and Abramson 1988a, 1988b; Davis 1997a, 1997b; Finkel, Guterbock, and Borg 1991; Hatchett and Schuman 1975–76; Schaeffer 1980; Schuman and Converse 1971; Schuman and Presser 1981; and Tucker 1983.

is true—that in saying that the white candidate should be admitted rather than the black, our black respondents are only saying what they think they are *supposed* to say: that the candidate with the highest score should be admitted. What would also have to be true? It would be silly to suggest that blacks will choose the black candidate over the white however large the difference between their admission scores whenever they are speaking to a fellow black. To believe that it makes some difference to blacks whether they are talking to blacks or whites does not require that you believe that it makes no difference to them how well (or poorly) a black candidate does on an admission test. All that is necessary is that, as the difference between the scores of the two candidates gets smaller, blacks will be increasingly likely to give the nod to the black candidate if they are talking to a fellow black.

As it happens, we kept track of which of our respondents was interviewed by a white interviewer and which by a black. And the results, shown in figure 4.9, are the exact opposite of the "masking" objection. When blacks are interviewed by a fellow black, they are *not* more likely to favor the black candidate as the difference between his score and that of the white candidate gets smaller. When the difference between the scores of the two is largest, more than eight out of ten choose the white candidate: and when it is smallest, again more than eight out of ten choose the white. Instructively, the increase in a tendency to choose the black candidate as the difference in admission scores decreases occurs when blacks are being interviewed by a *white* interviewer. When the difference is largest, fewer than one out of ten pick the black candidate; when it is smallest, one out of four do. Which means the "masking" objection gets reality exactly the wrong way around. It is not that blacks are more likely to tug their forelocks, so to speak, pretending to adopt the values of the "white" culture when they are speaking to a white. On the contrary, when they are talking to a white there is an inclination to engage, as it were, in a small act of racial defiance and make a point of saying that the black candidate should be admitted even though he has the lower score—despite the fact that their true attitude (which they presumably would express to a fellow black) is that whoever has the higher score should be admitted.

All of this, though, is about a difference at the margins. The results of the SAT experiment show that, whether they are being

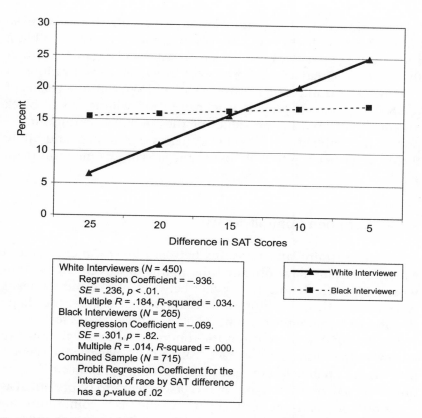

Figure 4.9. SAT Scores and Racial Favoritism by Race of Interviewer: Percent Favoring Admission of Black Applicant—Regression Lines

interviewed by a white or a black, the overriding rule that blacks follow is that the student who did better should be admitted. And they are overwhelmingly likely to follow this rule even when this requires not only that they say no to an applicant who is black, but to an applicant who is both black and from a disadvantaged background.

A few points need to be made by way of qualification. It is astonishing to us that these particular qualifications need to be expressly set out—they are no more than common sense suggests—but experience has taught us that it is better to do so than not. Perhaps most obviously, when we say that black Americans are ready to honor a principle even when it is to the disadvantage of black Americans to do so, we are *not* saying that blacks are indifferent to how well, or how poorly, other blacks fare. Nor are we saying that there is *no* point whatever at which differences in test scores between a black and a white applicant, however small, will be disregarded, or that there are no circumstances whatever in which considerations of race may not trump other considerations. That said, the results of the SAT experiment provide evidence of the willingness of black Americans to hold to the values of the American culture, interpreted and applied just as other Americans interpret and apply them, even when it is to their disadvantage as black Americans to do so.[136]

Common Commitments

The strains and divisions between black Americans and white Americans have obscured the points of agreement, of consensus, between them. The conflict between blacks and whites is real—we saw this in the previous chapter—but it takes the shape that it does because the consensus between them also is real.

The core of that consensus is the commitment to integration. We are aware that discussions of race from a black perspective suggest otherwise. In public forums, the principle of integration either goes unmentioned, or when notice of it is taken, tends to be presented as a position of a part—but only a part—of the black community, an ideal that in the optimistic years of the civil rights movement may have commanded the general support of blacks, but now is contested at the level of principle itself. And even where the principle of integration enjoys support, adherence to it is qualified by commitment to the competing values of black pride, black autonomy, and black self-respect. Integration is not a prominent item on the public agenda of black leaders or activists for more than one reason, but the danger of focusing on the views of activists is a general one, not peculiar to race. If you want to learn the views of ordinary citizens, of those who live in the world of everyday life, not the exceptional world of politics, you must take the trouble to ask them what they

[136] For an interesting study which emphasizes the convergence of black and white attitudes on aspects of affirmative action, but which unfortunately does not distinguish between considerations of academic merit and economic disadvantage in the experimental design, see Swain, Rodgers, and Silverman 2000.

think. You cannot simply assume that you know what they think because you know what others, including those who avowedly represent them, say that they think.

We suspected at the start that blacks are more committed to integration than is publicly acknowledged. The call for black power and racial separatism was at its height a generation ago. But in his classic study of protest and prejudice, Gary Marx had shown that the massive commitment of the black community was to integration even then.[137] Things now, we reasoned, would not be much different. But even believing that integration still was a primary value of black Americans, we were taken aback by what we found. It is not merely that integration is endorsed by a large number of blacks, not even that it is endorsed by the largest number of them. It is rather that, almost literally with the exception of only a relative handful, blacks reject racial separatism and instead support the ideal that people of different races should live and work together. And they not only support integration as a principle. They also overwhelmingly support integration as a strategy, rejecting racial separatism as a political route to racial equality, declaring instead that the best way to make real progress in achieving equality is for whites and blacks to work together.

It is indispensable, if one wishes to see things as they are, to recognize that black Americans are capable both of making a genuine commitment to a common American society and culture and of criticizing the racial inequalities that remain part of that society. They do see much that remains unfair. But they also, as the Life Chances experiment showed, overwhelmingly believe that America is a place where blacks and other minorities can make a good life.

Moreover, our results suggest that black and white Americans share a common culture. To point to a common culture is not to suggest that black Americans do not also have a sense of identity, traditions, practices, and views of the world that are distinctively theirs. Their experience in America has been unlike any other. They correspondingly have a sense of themselves, of their history, their concerns, their problems, as being unlike those of any other. And partly because of the burdens that uniquely have been imposed on them in the past, and partly because of the shoals that many find

---

[137] Marx 1967; see especially chaps. 1 and 5.

themselves stuck on now, black Americans have distinguished themselves by the extent of their commitment to a liberal, activist conception of government. But it does not follow either from having a distinct sense of self, or from having a distinctive political profile, that black Americans do not subscribe to core American values; to a shared understanding of what is right and wrong; to a common set of dilemmas in which the claims of core American values conflict one with another; to a consensual understanding that America should be a society in which considerations of race are secondary and not controlling. Our results point to a common set of commitments. Of the range of values that we have surveyed—law and order, individual freedom, the claims of religion and those of science—there is little cleavage between the commitments of black Americans and white Americans. No less important, it is not only a matter of blacks' adhering to the same values as whites, but also of their understanding these values in the same terms as do whites—even, and this does seem worth emphasis, when they pay a price for doing so. As the SAT experiment showed, black Americans do not merely give lip service to the value of achievement. They are ready to adhere to it even when it is to the disadvantage of fellow blacks. It would be a mistake to shortchange this evidence of the sincerity and the disinterestedness of black Americans' commitment to values common to all Americans.

In his classic, *An American Dilemma*, Gunnar Myrdal remarked that the issue of race is a problem in the heart of the American. He meant the white American.[138] But the issue inescapably is a problem in the heart of the black American, too. How is it possible to be black in America without weighing the American experience, without asking, How should I, as an American black, understand the American creed—the ideas of liberty, equality, and fair play, according to Myrdal—in a country that began in racial slavery and then enforced racial inequality? What should I, as a black, want to have in common with those who have wanted to have nothing in common with me? Do the claims of others, including those who also have suffered prejudice in America, compare with the unique burdens that blacks in America have had to bear? Can I—can one—identify with being black, take pride in the unique accomplishments of blacks, value what sets us distinctively apart from other Americans, and still identify wholeheartedly as an American?

We recognize that what we have to say about the views of black Americans is partial in at least two senses. It is partial in the sense of being incomplete. This is only one study. The ground that it covers is necessarily limited. But what we have to say also is partial in the sense of being limited by our perspective. We are white Americans writing about black Americans. That does not prevent what we say from being right. But it does mean that what we have seen, we have

---

[138] See Myrdal 1944, pp. li–lii. Myrdal's point was that white Americans held the power in America. The center of tension—between responsibility for the subjugation of black Americans and for living up to the creed—therefore was theirs.

seen from only one of a number of possible perspectives, black and white.

Our focus has been black pride. A sense of racial identification can express itself in an array of ways: in feeling a sense of identity and distinctiveness as a black in America; in insisting on the need to overcome the injustices of the past; in taking pride in the history blacks share and the works of all kinds they have accomplished; in wanting to promote an independent role for blacks to play as blacks, and on behalf of blacks; in insisting on recognition of the achievements of fellow blacks. We have sought to understand what these various forms of racial identification mean by exploring two questions. First, does being "pro-" black mean that blacks are more likely to be "anti-" those who are not black? Second, does having a distinctive identity as a black mean that blacks do not share a common ground, culture, and framework with other Americans?

We recognize that these are not the only important questions to ask about the politics of identity. And we understand now, in a way that we did not at the outset, that asking those questions raises others. But we believe now, as we believed then, that it is important to try to answer them.

I

Black emphasis on racial identity has been a concern of white Americans, liberal as well as conservative. But it has been a concern of black Americans, too, and for perfectly obvious reasons. Perfectly obvious because, whether it is black Americans or any other group, identification with your group can lead to rejection of other groups. Any number of headline clashes between blacks and other groups—Jews or Koreans or Latinos or whites—give credibility to the claim that black Americans are ready to rally around fellow blacks whatever their faults and react against others as though "only members of their own group should have any moral claim, or be entitled to political voice."[139]

Dramatic events notwithstanding, we believed that in the black community as a whole identifying with being black is not tied to

[139] Kiss 1996, p. 293.

rejecting others who are not black. Encouraged by the work of others,[140] as by our own studies of prejudice in a very different context,[141] this seemed to us the right hypothesis—or, if you prefer, guess—with which to start. But we recognized from the start that it might prove wrong, and we wanted to know what the truth of the matter was—are black pride and black intolerance related or not?—whatever the truth turned out to be. So we attacked the question at a variety of levels and in a number of ways.

Four lines of our findings are relevant. The first comes from the Switching the Beneficiary series of experiments. The idea behind these experiments, you will recall, was to take advantage of the power of randomized variations of questions to determine whether black Americans are as ready to support a given policy when a group other than blacks are the beneficiaries as when blacks are. So in one of these experiments we asked one half of our sample of black respondents whether they favored or opposed "large companies having quotas to make sure a certain number of blacks are hired," and asked the other half exactly the same question, except that we switched the beneficiaries to Mexican Americans.

Two features of these experiments are worth reemphasizing. First, the half who are being asked whether an affirmative action hiring plan should be set up to benefit African Americans has no way to figure out—and no reason at all to anticipate—that the other half are being asked whether the same should be done for Mexican Americans, and vice versa. An incentive merely to *appear* evenhanded is thus eliminated. Second, it would be understandable, quite apart from whether it strictly is justifiable or not, if African Americans took the position that affirmative action is a policy on which they have a special claim. Yet as this experiment (and another designed to test the reliability of the results of the first) showed, a virtually identical proportion of black Americans supported the affirmative action plan set up to help Mexican Americans as supported the one set up to help fellow black Americans.

It is true that the intensity of support is greater when blacks are to benefit. And it also is true that we cannot tell the exact reasoning that lies behind the similarity of choices in the two conditions.

---

[140] See especially Brewer 2001.
[141] See Sniderman et al. 2000.

Black Americans, for example, may be as ready to support affirmative action for Mexican Americans, not because they believe Mexican Americans are entitled to it, but rather because they figure that the chances of affirmative action surviving and continuing to benefit blacks are better if a broader coalition benefits from it. This possibility doesn't square with our own sense of the findings all in all, and there is no direct evidence in favor of it, but it nonetheless is a logical possibility.

These caveats notwithstanding, what we observe is that black Americans are as likely to support affirmative action when someone else benefits as when they do. This line of results thus suggests that black Americans do not make political choices on the basis of an ingroup-outgroup calculus, supporting a policy if they are the beneficiaries, opposing it if another group is to benefit.

A second line of results addresses the question of whether there is a connection between blacks' identifying with being black and their readiness to be intolerant of others—notably, Jews. The issue of black anti-Semitism is highly charged. So in attempting to measure black attitudes toward Jews, we did not make use of questions of our own devising. Instead, we employed questions used as the standard indicators of anti-Semitism over the last forty years.[142] The more difficult problem was defining racial identification, since the danger— of artifactually creating a relationship between taking pride in being black and being anti-Semitic—becomes more likely if one arbitrarily picks a definition of black racial identification.

The best, the only, way to avoid the trap of arbitrary definition is to follow the lead of previous researchers, who have distinguished a number of different senses of racial identification, emphasizing two in particular. Most obviously, there is the criterion of feeling a sense of racial solidarity. But of what, it must be asked, does this sense of solidarity consist? Not, or at any rate not merely, in a feeling of closeness or kinship with fellow blacks. What is involved is more substantial. It is a belief in genuine interconnectedness, a sense of a direct connection between other blacks and oneself, so that what happens to other blacks bears on what happens to one as a black. So conceived, a feeling of racial solidarity centers on a conviction that

---

[142] As a reminder, although the wording of the questions was virtually identical, the response format was not; see chapter 3.

black Americans, by virtue of being black in America, share a common fate.

Another element of racial identification emphasized in previous work is the desire of black Americans to exercise a greater measure of control over their future. Depending on chance and circumstance, this aspiration for a larger say by blacks over their future can take a variety of forms. It lies, for example, behind support for schools that would enroll only young black men. It grounds a belief that black Americans should have control over government in communities where blacks make up a majority.[143] It also finds expression in the views that black Americans should have control over the economy in mostly black neighborhoods and that blacks should shop in stores owned by other blacks whenever possible.

These and similar expressions of a desire for a greater measure of control have sometimes been labeled "black nationalism." Yet a "nationalist" label is somewhat misleading. Studies over the last forty years have made plain that the overwhelming number of black Americans reject actual nationalism in the sense of the establishment of an independent black, territorial nation-state.[144] Still, there is no question that black Americans have a sense of forming a distinct body of people, sharing a history of suffering and accomplishment that gives them a unique identity and perspective. And an integral element of this sense of collective identity is a belief that the interests and prospects of blacks not just as individuals, but as black Americans, are and ought to be the object of concern. A desire for greater autonomy for blacks is not the same as a quest for total black political autonomy, but it has, as a part of its distinctive tone, a collective dimension, and not simply an individual one. Blacks of course want to exercise a greater degree of control over their own lives. But they also wish blacks to have a greater say over the lives of blacks as a group.

To these two elements of racial identification—a feeling of soli-

---

[143] See Dawson 2001, table A3.2, p. 363, for components of his measure of Black Autonomy.

[144] For a reading in the mid-1960s, see Marx 1967, table 2, p. 28, who finds support for a separate black nation ranging from 16 percent to 26 percent in his four-city sample. See Dawson 2001, table A.1, p. 327, who finds support of 14 percent in his national sample thirty years later. Note that the wording of the questions in the two surveys, though similar, is not identical.

darity and an aspiration for a greater measure of autonomy—we added a third: a desire that the achievements of blacks be properly acknowledged. As a practical matter, we assessed this third element in two different ways: by gauging the importance that blacks attach to building black pride and self-respect, and by measuring their support for a popular version of Afrocentrism asserting that Western philosophy and science really were rooted in African achievements.

For us the important question is whether valuing a sense of distinctiveness as a black American goes along in any significant degree with a willingness to deprecate other groups that are not blacks, especially Jews. Our answer, with one qualification, is no. We can find no connection of any consequence between black Americans' readiness to be prejudiced against Jews and their feeling a sense of solidarity with fellow blacks, desire to build up black pride and self-respect, or aspiration to increase black Americans' measure of economic autonomy. We do, it is true, find a relationship between support for Afrocentrism and black anti-Semitism, and although that relationship is not very strong, it persists even after a number of other factors are taken into account. Our principal finding, however, is that other forms of racial identification only appear to be related to anti-Semitism because they are related to Afrocentrism.

A third line of findings brings to bear evidence based on randomized experiments (as opposed to merely correlational analyses). A number of our findings are relevant, but we would like to underscore particularly the results of two sets of experiments. The first is the College Editor experiment. In that experiment, as you may recall, one random half of our respondents were asked whether a Jewish editor of a college newspaper, who had published an article critical of black students, should be fired. The other half were asked the same question exactly the other way around—namely, whether a black editor of a college newspaper who had published an article critical of Jewish students should be fired.

Here surely one might think that blacks may take offense at the Jewish editor, especially if they identify with their fellow blacks. Who should be more sensitive to a suggestion that blacks are being disrespected, one may reason, than a black who feels a sense of solidarity with other blacks and believes it important to build black pride and self-respect?

It is true that the more strongly that blacks feel some forms of racial identification—for example, a desire that blacks have more autonomy and control—the more likely they are to rally around the *black* editor and oppose his being fired. But with one exception only, there is no relationship between the variety of ways of taking pride in being black we have assessed and the readiness of blacks to favor firing the *Jewish* editor, the exception again being Afrocentrism.

The second experiment we want to underscore is the Blanket Charges of Racism experiment. This experiment, you will remember, was set up to test how ready African Americans are to issue a blanket charge of racism against some other group. It is not without interest, we admit, to learn that about one in every four blacks is ready to charge most of another group with being racist. Depending on your perspective, this number is either reassuringly small or distressingly large. And it also is of interest to learn that blacks are somewhat more likely to allege that most whites are racist than that most Jews are. But neither of these results goes to the heart of the matter. What is of importance is what leads some blacks, but not others, to issue blanket charges of racism against other groups.

Given the history of racism in America, it may seem only common sense that the more strongly black Americans identify with fellow blacks the more likely they would be to see other groups in America as racist. If so, some or all of the forms of racial identification we have canvassed—a desire to see blacks exercise more control over their economic future, a feeling of sharing a common fate, a desire to build black pride, an insistence on the historic accomplishments of Africans—will encourage a readiness to believe that others are racist. But our results show no evidence of this. Taking pride in being black and in black history does not encourage blacks to believe that others are racist. The answer is quite different. It is black intolerance—specifically, black anti-Semitism—not black pride that encourages blacks to issues blanket charges of racism against others. In a word, what encourages blacks to believe that others are prejudiced against them is their being prejudiced against others.

The fourth and final line of evidence concerns the reactions of blacks to fellow blacks. We have seen that most of the forms of identifying with being black—feeling a sense of solidarity with fellow blacks, wishing to build black pride, and wanting blacks to have a greater measure of control over their economic future—do not lead blacks to think ill of those who are not black. But clashes between black activists and other minorities have captured so much public attention because taking pride in being black pride and rejecting those who are not black appear to be braided together. So the all-important question is whether black intolerance encourages black solidarity in the larger black community.

The results of the Immigrant Tax Burden experiment are especially telling on this score. In this experiment we ask all of our respondents whether the arrival of immigrants from another country into the United States is likely to cause taxes to increase. But, entirely at random, one-third of the time we identify the immigrants as Mexicans and other Hispanics, another third of the time as Koreans and other Asians, and the final third of the time as immigrants from countries in Africa. The question is, if our respondents are prejudiced what difference will that make in the likelihood they will say that immigrants are going to be a burden?

Naturally—it would be astonishing otherwise—the more prejudiced blacks are, the more likely they are to say that Latino immigrants and Asian immigrants are going to cause taxes to increase. But what is more interesting, and a good deal less obvious, is that the more prejudiced blacks are, the more likely they are to say that immigrants from Africa also will be a tax burden. The lesson is worth underlining. To think ill of members of other groups inclines you to think ill, not well, of members of your own.[145]

Each of these four lines of findings, it should be needless to say, has limits. But they all point in the same direction. And that gives us confidence in the conclusion to draw. Whatever is true of black activists, in the larger black community being problack does not mean being antiwhite—or anti-Jewish, or anti-Hispanic, or anti-Asian. Black pride and black prejudice are *not* opposite sides of the same coin

II

An issue that we did not set out to address, but which emerged from our study's results, is black Americans' standards of critical judgment on some matters of race. Consider Afrocentrism.

---

[145] See Sniderman et al. 2000 for cross-validation in the case of Italians: the more likely they are to think ill of immigrants, the more likely they are to think ill of their fellow Italians; pp. 85–89. See also n. 97 in this volume.

The heart of the matter is the claim that two of the pillars of European civilization, modern science and philosophy, actually have their roots in African civilization.[146] There of course is a rich set of intellectual connections between European civilization and other civilizations, very much including Egyptian civilization and also that of Africa more broadly. But it is one thing to trace a skein of influences in the history of ideas. It is quite another to claim that "African wise men who lived hundreds of years ago do not get enough credit for their contributions to modern science" or that "the ancient Greek philosophers copied many ideas from black philosophers who lived in Egypt." And very large numbers of ordinary blacks in our study, as we have seen, agree with each claim— and on the order of two out of every three agree (at least somewhat) with both. They subscribe to both in spite of the fact that each, on its face, invites a critical evaluation. African wise men may have made contributions on a variety of fronts, but it is not obvious what they have contributed to modern science. And as for the suggestion that ancient Greek philosophers "copied" their ideas from black Egyptian predecessors, it beggars belief to suppose that substantial numbers of a sample of average citizens, white or black, would have any definite idea who these ancient Greek philosophers were, let alone any grounded notion of what ideas they might have filched.

One of course could reply that these claims of the contributions of ancient Africans to modern civilization represent only the harmless exaggeration commonplace in ordinary conversation. If people were to say only what is strictly true, hardly anybody would have much to say. And in any case isn't it pettifogging to construe these issues so narrowly? Isn't it more reasonable to suppose that what really is being said is that all too often the contributions of blacks have not been properly credited and that these two particular examples, of African contributions to philosophy and science, just stand as examples (or metaphors) of the larger point at issue?

There is an element of validity to these deflationary responses. But Afrocentrism, at any rate in its popular version, has at its core the notion that whites are actively resistant to honoring black achievement and that they will go to some lengths to cover up their indebtedness to black accomplishments. Hence the appeal of

---

[146] The preeminent source for this claim is Bernal 1987.

diffuse suggestions that Greek philosophers have taken credit for ideas that really were developed by their African predecessors and that modern science has not acknowledged the debt it owes to African wise men. Moreover Afrocentrism is only one expression of a conspiratorial strain in black thinking, and in addition is, as we have seen, closely tied to ideas about vast, ongoing conspiracies against blacks.

In this study, we looked at two of these conspiratorial beliefs— that "the FBI and the CIA make sure that there is a steady supply of guns and drugs in the inner city" and that "white doctors created the AIDS virus in a laboratory and released it into black neighbor- hoods." What, one must ask, does this readiness to believe in a variety of cover-ups and conspiracies say about the character of thought in the larger black community?

In this era of popular psychology, it surely is tempting to surmise that a paranoid personality lies behind a readiness to allege such conspiracies. We know of no evidence, however, that supports this interpretation, and at several points in our study we have seen results that contradict it. The overlap between believing in racial cover-ups and our measures of psychological mistrust or lack of self-esteem is not significant. And nothing in our results indicates that endorsing these conspiratorial ideas is connected to being socially marginal. Moreover, when it comes at least to some of these ideas, it is not those who are the least educated, the worst-off, or the most ill-informed politically who are most likely to embrace them; on the contrary, it is those who have had the most education, are the best-off, and are the most politically sophisticated.

One might of course go on to say that blacks believe vast con- spiracies continue to be carried out against them because there have been so many carried out against them in the past, and that the better educated or more politically engaged blacks are, the more likely they are to know of these conspiracies that are part of the black experience in America. From this perspective, it is not necessary to defend the literal truth, for example, of the claim that white doctors created AIDS and then released it to eliminate blacks, although some have claimed to have evidence of FBI and CIA involvement in supplying drugs and guns in black ghettoes. The relevant point is quite different. It is only that it is not unreason- able, let alone irrational, for black Americans to take seriously the idea of racial conspiracies given the historical record of actual wrongs done to blacks.

The suggestion that the thinking of blacks needs to be understood against the background of history has obvious merit. Thus, by way of explaining the overlap between support for black autonomy and a belief that AIDS was created as the result of an antiblack conspiracy, it has been contended that "the consistent revelations about government misdeeds in the black community ranging from the medical crimes of the Tuskegee experiments, the FBI's COINTELPRO operations of the Civil Rights and Black Power era, and the wide coverage of possible CIA involvement in crack distribution in the black community periodically serve to reinforce the belief in such conspiracies across a wide range of African Americans who hold a variety of ideological orientations."[147]

Certainly, atrocities have been committed against blacks; certainly also, one reason ordinary blacks believe that they continue to be committed is because some black elites and black media claim that they continue to be committed. But it is not sufficient to brush aside a readiness by blacks to allege the particular conspiracies that we have picked out in part because they are only examples of a continually expanding pool of claims made by black Americans of vast, contemporary conspiracies being carried out against them. Patricia Turner, for example, begins her study of rumor in the black community by listing a host of other claims, running from claims that the Ku Klux Klan owns Church's fast food chicken franchise "and they put something in it to make black men sterile;" to allegations that "the killings [of twenty-eight African Americans] in Atlanta were related to genocide of the black race . . . (and) the FBI was responsible and using the bodies for interferon research;" to "Reebok is made in South Africa . . . (and) all of the money they make off of those shoes goes to support whites in South Africa."[148] There is, in short, a readiness not just to find particular claims of conspiracy credible read against the specific background of black experience— as the claim of AIDS might in some sense be credible when read against the background of the Tuskegee research—but instead a willingness to find credible virtually any conceivable claim of conspir-

[147] Dawson 2001, p. 131.
[148] Turner 1993, pp. 2–3. For an update on still more rumors and conspiracies, both black and white, see Fine and Turner 2001.

acy. Besides, it is not much of an explanation to say that black Americans are ready to charge that vast conspiracies to harm them continue to be carried out now because other conspiracies were carried out earlier. It is simply not true that black Americans uniformly give credence to the kinds of fantastic charges we have examined. And that means it is necessary to find out why some blacks find these claims credible while others do not.

Another consideration is still more important. Being ready to believe in conspiracies matters because we have seen that it increases a susceptibility to prejudice. Comparing levels of agreement with negative stereotypes of Jews, using both our national and Chicago samples, we found the levels of anti-Semitism to be significantly higher among black Americans than white Americans—a result cross-validated by two independent studies using national samples of black and white Americans. Our own data indicate that the same major factors are responsible for anti-Semitism among black Americans as among white Americans. But our data also suggest that anti-Semitism is further increased among blacks by a medley of conspiratorial and rejectionist sentiments that include Afrocentrism, beliefs in racial conspiracies, and support for Louis Farrakhan and the Black Muslims. The individuals and institutions in the black community that legitimize and strengthen conspiratorial thinking among black Americans legitimize and strengthen closed-mindedness and intolerance.

And this matters more broadly because Afrocentrism certainly, and conspiratorial thinking to a lesser extent, are connected to a larger set of ideas about racial identity. It is important, therefore, to ask how an idea like Afrocentrism comes to be connected to ideas like racial solidarity, a desire to build black pride, or a belief in the importance of increasing black economic autonomy, and what are the consequences of this interconnection.

In a seminal article on the organization of political thinking, Philip Converse identified different ways that individual ideas can be constrained together to form larger political perspectives.[149] The rules of logic, for example, can supply one type of constraint. Citizens, having accepted certain premises, may derive their logical implications in a step-by-step deductive process. Some unusual individuals may put together idea systems through such deductive rea-

---

[149] Converse 1964.

soning under some exceptional circumstances. But it is fantasy to suppose that ordinary citizens are in the habit of organizing their ideas about politics through the abstract machinery of deductive reasoning, and, in any case, no chain of logically necessary connections requires that blacks who believe that black Americans should, for example, have more say over the economic lives of their communities must also believe that modern science has not acknowledged its debt to African wise men. It is a historically contingent fact, not a logically necessary one, that a desire for economic autonomy and a belief in Afrocentrism are components of the current package of ideas about black solidarity.

Psychological consistency is an alternative to logical consistency. Individual ideas may be bound together to form, from the perspective of the person who holds them, a coherent whole, and what gives them coherence is that they express a common underlying psychological affect or need. An explanation along these lines may appear an obvious candidate to explain how the various forms of racial identification we have examined are related. Think of what they are: a desire to have more autonomy; a sense of sharing a common fate with other blacks; a decision to insist on recognition of the historic accomplishments of blacks; and a belief about the importance of strengthening black pride and self-esteem. All can be seen as ways of strengthening a person's own sense of value.

This is the premise of the now familiar argument that groups who have been subordinated and whose history has been demeaned, ignored, or misrepresented should have their accomplishments and struggles acknowledged and honored by the larger society. When the issue of racial identity is put in the context of the sufferings of blacks in the American experience, it is natural—indeed, it may even appear self-evident—that black pride offers a balm for wounds to black self-esteem. And just so far as different forms of racial identification represent a common way to compensate for wounded self-esteem, it would seem natural that they should form a common package. Because this has seemed so self-evidently right, it is the more important to observe that our results fail to support it. In our study, we can find no relationship of any consequence between the level of support blacks give to expressions of black pride, whatever the specific form of expressing pride, and their level of personal self-esteem. The notion of therapeutic politics is deeply entrenched, so it is worth underscoring that the results of an independent study, conducted at approximately the same time and using measures comparable to ours, are virtually identical with our own.[150]

It is not always recognized that the suggestion that black Americans lack self-esteem is patronizing.[151] Our findings thus offer some protection against the temptation to view the politics of identity as a vehicle of personal therapy. Issues of black identity and racial pride, our results suggest, are rooted not in the interior psychology of black Americans, but in the history and tensions of American politics.

But if neither logical nor psychological sources bind together the variety of orientations to race that we have canvassed, what does? A third alternative is shared interests. People may, and sometimes do, embrace ideas as a coherent whole, not because of any intellectual or emotional connection between these different ideas, but because it is to their advantage to believe each, and thus to their advantage to hold all.

Self-interest is part of politics, including racial politics. But we have not been able to uncover a systematic connection between the assemblage of ideas about racial identity and solidarity that we have examined and a distinct set of economic interests in the larger black community. It is true that a desire for blacks to control more businesses in black neighborhoods and for fellow blacks to patronize them wins more support from better-off blacks than from poorly-off ones. But that is the only element of the larger package for which we can find a tie to economic advantage. Otherwise, racial identification only appears to be tied to income because income is tied to education. One could of course reply that, as a general proposition, blacks will benefit the more ground that ideas of black solidarity gain; and there no doubt is some truth to this. The difficulty is not that this kind of explanation fails to explain anything. On the contrary, the difficulty is that it explains too much. It gives a reason for blacks—for any and every black—to favor emphasizing his or her racial identity but, as we have seen, blacks vary a good deal in how much emphasis they give to their racial identity. In any case, what is needed is to understand how the contemporary package of ideas about racial identity has been formed. Afrocentrism is part of the

[150] See discussion, chap. 2.
[151] For a thoughtful, encompassing, and nuanced exposition of this position, see Scott 1997.

package of ideas about racial identity and pride now in general circulation in the larger black community. Blacks who feel they share a common fate with other blacks are more likely to support Afrocentrism than are blacks who do not feel that what happens to other blacks has a large impact on what happens to them. The same applies to blacks who attach a special importance to building black pride or to increasing blacks' control over their economic future. And the same applies, to a lesser extent, to embracing ideas of racial conspiracies. Each of these elements is tied to the others. Accepting one increases the likelihood that each of the others will be accepted as well.

The crucial question is, how do political ideas come to be tied or connected to other ideas to form an overall package? The best answer is bipartite. The first part has to do with the role of political elites, including media elites. They organize political ideas, defining what goes with what. And it is because ideas come in organized packages that if ordinary citizens accept one idea from a package, they are more likely to accept others. The second part has to do with the diffusion of ideas. All citizens are not equally well positioned to learn which ideas currently go with which others; and it is the best-educated and most politically aware segments of the general public who are best able to recognize what goes with what.

The braiding of ideas that are simplistic and conspiratorial, such as Afrocentrism, with more traditional forms of group identification, such as a sense of common fate, is the core of what has come to concern us. The elaboration and popularization of Afrocentrism is the work of certain black activists and intellectuals, while many black leaders and the black media have given legitimacy and publicity to an array of rumors and allegations of conspiracies, running from government drug rings to the creation of AIDS in order to destroy blacks. The result has been to tie what Richard Hofstadter, writing of the fevered politics of the 1950s, characterized as the paranoid style, to a broader range of ideas about racial identity and pride.[152] This has more than one consequence, but the most important, we have become persuaded, is the blunting of the standards and habits of critical judgment in the larger black community.

Here, very briefly, is the background provided by previous studies.

[152] Hofstadter 1967.

First, better-educated black Americans are more likely to be exposed to the black print and visual media. Second, better-educated blacks are more likely to pick up the overall package of ideas about racial identity and solidarity because of their greater exposure to black print and visual media.[153] Our own results confirm that the more educated blacks are, the more likely they are to embrace all of the principal ideas in this package: racial solidarity, building black pride, greater economic autonomy, and also Afrocentrism. The crux of the matter then becomes, what is the effect of embracing a package of ideas, one part of which is marked by a paranoid style?

Education is the social institution that most directly and significantly inculcates the cognitive skills and intellectual orientations necessary for critical thinking. The more education that people have had, the better able they are to assess the validity of claims made to them, to judge whether supportive evidence is being offered on their behalf, to assess whether this evidence is overly broad, vague, or open to obvious objections. Indeed, the connection between the amount of education that people have had a chance to obtain and their facility in critical thinking is so close that Selznick and Steinberg, in their classic study of prejudice, declared that the lack of education leads to "cognitive simplism."[154]

Education, in a word, inculcates the intellectual skills and habits of critical thinking. And one of the most important benefits of critical thinking is to make citizens, black or white, less vulnerable to distorted claims about evil intent and phantom conspiracies. The problem, our findings suggest, is that for black Americans the advantage that education confers in applying standards of critical thinking is offset by the advantage that it confers in keeping up with current ideas, with being au courant. Thus better-educated blacks are, by virtue of being so, more likely to pick up ideas about black pride now in circulation, one of which is Afrocentrism. But just so far as they give credence to some of the claims of the Afrocentrism, they lose part—not all—of the benefits of critical thinking that accompany more substantial education.

The problem of anti-Semitism offers one illustration of this blunting of critical standards. As a general rule, the better educated citizens are, the more resistant they are to oversimplified, exaggerated ideas, very much including the oversimplifications involved in prej-

---

[153] See especially Allen, Dawson, and Brown 1989.
[154] See Selznick and Steinberg 1969.

udice. This holds for black Americans as for white Americans, with one complication. On the one side, by virtue of being more educated, blacks are more likely to reject the exaggerations and oversimplifications of group stereotypes; on the other side, by virtue of being more likely to embrace Afrocentrism, better-educated blacks are more likely to accept the simplifications of stereotypes of Jews. Both effects are real, and since they are approximately equal in strength, each tends to cancel out the other. The result is to blunt the advantage in critical thinking that education usually confers. Better-educated blacks are not more likely to accept negative stereotypes of Jews. But neither are they markedly more likely to reject them. The same blunting of critical standards applies to conspiratorial thinking. Well-educated blacks are not markedly more likely to accept the claim that the AIDS virus, for instance, was invented by white doctors and released in black neighborhoods. But neither are they markedly more likely to reject it.

These are results that can be demonstrated in our data. What cannot be demonstrated with our data is a broader vulnerability of the larger black community. From an outsider's perspective, it is impressive to observe the power of black leaders to rally support from the black community by appeals to the need for racial solidarity and allegations of conspiracies against them directed by one or another agency of the government. There certainly is nothing unique to the black experience in this. Other groups, at these and other times, are and have been susceptible to elite manipulation. But our concern here is with black Americans, and it is hard to escape the suspicion that the blunting of standards of critical judgment on some matters of race opens up the larger black community to manipulation. To say by way of expiation that, because there were infamous medical experiments in Tuskegee sixty years ago, it is reasonable for black Americans to believe that white doctors have developed AIDS in order to commit racial genocide is to say that black elites have a license to invent, and black citizens a right to believe, almost any allegation whatever. Irrationalism on this scale does not come free.

III

An important line of black political thought is dedicated to the cultural and intellectual independence of black America. In one version or another and at one time or another, this idea has been a theme, for example, of W. E. B. Du Bois;[155] Marcus Garvey, through his leadership of the Universal Negro Improvement Association;[156] Richard Wright, in the service of a dialectic of (ultimate) transcendence;[157] Malcolm X, until the last period of his life;[158] Elijah Muhammad and Louis Farrakhan insistently and throughout their careers;[159] Huey Newton, on behalf of the Black Panther Movement; and a number of others, on behalf of the Black Power Movement more generally;[160] and most recently, Molefi Asanti,[161] Leonard Jeffries, Ron Karenga,[162] and other spokesmen for Afrocentricity.[163] On the view of all of those individuals, even if race is only a social construction, race is not just a construction of whites imposed on blacks. It is as importantly a construction of blacks, reflecting their identity, their culture, their sense of self—and therefore deserving of their support. Viewed from this perspective, at a fundamental level Black America is separate from, independent of, even at crucial points at odds with, the larger American culture.

There is no question about the strength of racial identity among black Americans; nor about the depth of their differences with white Americans over issues of race—over how much racial inequality remains, why it persists, and what should be done about it.[164] But what our findings demonstrate is that developing and enjoying a sense of identity as black Americans does not undercut or attenuate the identity of blacks as Americans. The whole thrust of our findings is that, in their fundamental values and outlook, black Americans are Americans.

To say this is not at all to say that every American black and white has the same values. It is instead to say that white and black Americans tend to be caught up in the same way by the conflicts of values that give individual lives their distinctive moral shape and, what is

---

[155] Lewis 1993, 2000.
[156] Cronon 1969.
[157] Malcomson 2000, p. 242.
[158] Dawson 2001, pp. 102–3.
[159] Evanzz 1999.
[160] Pearson 1994.
[161] Banks 1996.
[162] Dawson 2001, pp. 107–8.
[163] Howe 1998; Lefkowitz 1996; Walker 2001.
[164] Kinder and Winter 2001.

more, that they tend to resolve these conflicts as individuals, and not as people who are either black or white. It is not, after all, a matter of either being in favor of law and order or in favor of individual freedom—who believes in the one without also wishing to believe in the other? The whole problem, the reason why there is a moral judgment to make, is because it sometimes is necessary to balance the relative importance of the one value against that of the other. And when it comes to making choices between competing values, what stands out is the commonality, not the divergence, between the choices that black and white Americans make.

It would be an oversimplification to frame the question of sharing a common culture in categorical terms, as though the choices that any two groups make within a country must be identical at every point or else each necessarily adheres to its own culture—separate, distinct, and independent of the other. There are differences of degree and emphasis in belief and outlook between black Americans and other Americans, as there no doubt are between, for example, Jewish Americans and Hispanic Americans. What has struck us, however, is how small the differences between black and white Americans are in the values we have explored, including values like the importance attached to religion, that have commonly been supposed to be especially characteristic of black Americans.

It may be objected that a commonality of values at this level misses the point. To contend that black Americans stand apart from the common culture is not to claim that they share no values with other Americans. It is rather to claim that a significant part of black Americans' sense of what is fair inescapably reflects their struggle for racial justice, and that in the arena of this struggle, their judgment as to what is fair both does, and should, differ from that of white Americans.

There is a sense in which this is true, but it is important to be clear just what exactly this sense is. Black Americans, on average, take a different position than white Americans on what government should do for minorities. They also, again on average, have quite different beliefs than white Americans about the extent of discrimination that persists, the limits to equal opportunity that remain, and the harassment and indignities that black Americans continue to experience. All of this is true, and to say that it is all about politics is not to say that it is in any respect unimportant. But the deepest differences we have observed between white and black Americans are about politics. In politics, points of disagreement are at the natural center of attention. And what has happened is that these points of differences have been generalized and exaggerated and taken as evidence that there are two separate cultures in America—one white, one black.

But the focus on disagreement between black and white Americans has obscured the encompassing areas of agreement. Indeed, the full range of evidence suggests that black and white Americans share a common culture, framework, and understanding of core values.

Previous studies have shown that blacks overwhelmingly repudiate separatism. When the idea of separatism is put in expressly political terms, black Americans reject by a massive margin the proposition that black Americans should have their own separate nation.[165] But it is not only the political fantasy of a black nation-state that is confined to the margins of the black community. So, too, is the idea of severing the ties of everyday life with their fellow citizens, white Americans. Quite simply, the idea that they "should have nothing to do with whites" is almost entirely without support.[166] And it is not just extreme versions of separatism that are rejected. Even expressions of racial separatism that may seem no more than strategic politics tend to be confined to a minority. So by a clear margin, black Americans reject the notion that blacks should whenever possible vote for black candidates.[167]

We have found the occasional result that differs from those of our study.[168] But these are exceptions, not only to our results but to those of other studies, too.[169] The balance of the evidence is clear. Most black Americans reject separatism. But in reviewing previous studies while preparing for our own, we wondered exactly what

[165] Dawson reports that only 14 percent nationally agree that black people should have their own separate nation; 86 percent disagree; see Dawson 2001, p. 327.

[166] Dawson 1994, p. 191.

[167] Dawson 1994, p. 190. Dawson, in *Black Visions*, finds in one survey that one-half support a separate black party, but as best we can tell, this is a one-time observation and not matched by the other indicators of black separatism in Dawson's own study, which correspond to our own.

[168] The major exceptions are several results from the 1994 National Black Politics Study, which suggest more support for some forms of black-focused commitments (for example whether blacks should form their own political party and whether blacks form a nation within a nation); see Dawson 2001, table A1.1, pp. 327–28.

[169] See Triandis 1976, 1988.

moral to draw. It is one thing for black Americans to reject separatism—to reject, as it were, the idea of rejecting white Americans. But it is another thing for them positively to affirm a common fellowship with white Americans. To what extent, we asked, do black Americans share ground, a common culture, with their fellow Americans? To what extent do they want to share this ground?

The ideals that black Americans accept—and not just those that they reject—seemed to us worth the effort to grasp. Our values say something important about who we are, as Isaiah Berlin taught, because, at one time or another, they will collide with one another.[170] And what we choose, when we must choose, reveals what we most truly value.

The importance of forcing our respondents to choose between two goals, each of which is of value in its own right, impressed itself upon us. It would be of interest to see that most blacks favor integration, considered in isolation from any competing consideration. But it would carry more weight, we reasoned, to learn that black Americans, if asked to choose between the desirability of blacks living together with fellow blacks or living together with whites, choose the ideal of integration over that of racial solidarity.

And black Americans do choose in favor of integration systematically, consistently. Think of some of our specific findings and of the larger implications that follow from them. It is perfectly clear that the largest number of our respondents have a distinct sense of being black, of belonging to a distinctively black culture, and of taking pride in both. But it also is true, and worth extreme emphasis, that when they are asked which is more important, to emphasize what Americans have in common or to promote black culture as a separate culture, we saw that by a clear margin they choose what we as Americans, black and white, have in common as the more important. Or think of the ideal of integration. At its high water mark, the civil rights movement committed itself not merely to the dismantling of racial segregation, but to the establishment of an America where all could find their place regardless of the color of their skin. As the movement lost momentum, however, a new generation of black leaders rose to challenge the leadership not just of white America but of black America, as well. And the challenge went to the

---

[170] The classic presentation of this position is Berlin 1969.

ideals of the movement, as well the leadership. Integration, the argument went, meant assimilation. So viewed, the civil rights movement, in Adolph Reed's words, stood for "cultural homogenization," for seeing that "the Negro be thought of as 'any other American'"; for "the same 'eradication of otherness' that had been forced upon immigrant populations."[171] And since the rise of the black power movement and its lineal descendant, Afrocentricity, the ideal of integration has been eclipsed in black political rhetoric.[172]

Yet the insistence of black political rhetoric notwithstanding, our findings suggest that the convictions of ordinary black Americans are quite different. Asked to say whether blacks are better off living with whites or living with other blacks in black neighborhoods, we saw that a large majority of our black respondents choose in favor of integration. Just as important, our results show that there is a consensus in the larger black community that, to make real progress in achieving equality, it is better for blacks to work together with whites than to work together mostly with other blacks. For that matter, asked to choose which is more important, helping those who are worse-off regardless of their color or concentrating on helping blacks, by a one-sided margin they favor helping those who are worse-off regardless of color. Cutting across the divide of race is their ideal and, in their view, the ideal way to achieve their ideal.

We ourselves began with the belief that black and white Americans share the same culture. And just because this was our view, we wanted to assess, in as demanding a way as possible, whether black Americans are genuinely committed to core American values. And when we speak of support for core values, we do not mean just being willing to say that you believe in a particular principle, but of being ready to stick to it when you have to pay a price for doing so.

Thus the SAT experiment. The aim, you will recall, was to determine how black Americans weigh the claims of racial justice and a commitment to the standard of achievement when they conflict. They were asked which of two young men a college should admit, if it could only admit one. One of the young men, George, was black; the other, Sam, was white. Sam, they were told, scored higher on his college entrance exam than George. Which of the young men, they

[171] Reed 1999, p. 65.
[172] Ibid., 1999, p. 217.

were asked, should be admitted: George, "because of the special obstacles faced by blacks," or Sam, whose is score on the entrance exam was higher?

The crucial characteristic of the SAT experiment, the feature that made it unusual, was that the size of the difference between their exam scores was randomly varied. Sometimes it was very large, sometimes moderate, sometimes very small. The reason for varying the size of the difference in exam scores was to find the point at which, in the judgment of black Americans, the difference did not matter when the needs of racial justice were taken into account.

We want to say again that everybody who knew about this experiment, ourselves very much included, agreed that at some point the majority of our black respondents would choose the black candidate for admission. So when we say the results of the SAT experiment are surprising, we are saying that they surprised us, too. For the fact of the matter is that when the difference in scores was large, nine out of every ten of our respondents picked the white candidate: yet when it was very small, eight out of every ten still did exactly the same. And what this means is that when blacks say they are committed to achievement, they really are committed to it. For they not only favor it in the abstract, they make it the decisive principle even when doing so comes at the expense of a fellow black. It is time to retire the idea that you can tell whether Americans are committed to core American values just by knowing the color of their skin.

IV

One theme of recent research has been black Americans' sense of a separate identity and their creation of a distinct political culture.[173] Another has been their embitterment and rejection of the American dream because of their failure to be given a fair opportunity to achieve it.[174] But although arguing from different premises, the one focusing on black Americans' sense of distinctiveness, the other on their disillusionment with the American dream, they come to a common point: the alienation of black Americans, the growing

[173] A paradigmatic example is Dawson 2001.
[174] The seminal presentation of this view is Hochschild 1995.

separation between black and white Americans. The picture is one of blacks turning inward, having lost confidence in the promise of America, drawing on their unique experience and traditions to develop their own ideas and aspirations.

This vision of a Black America—separate, distinct, committed to its own goals and self-conception—appeals to activists and intellectuals both black and white. But it is a vision that obscures the commitments of black Americans. Without at all minimizing the conviction of many black Americans that racism remains a major problem in American life, or the sentiments that follow on the heels of this conviction, our findings persuade us that black Americans share a common culture, a common set of values, with white Americans.

We recognize that to some this is a provocative claim. From the point of view of some black American intellectuals, to suggest that black Americans as a whole are—and wish to be—part of the larger American culture signals a lack of respect for black culture.[175] On their view, for black Americans to be as American as white Americans, they must "assimilate" to the values and principles of a culture other than their own. On our view, it is an irony worth consideration that some blacks now suggest that black Americans as a group stand outside of American history and culture, as though, after all of this time and struggle and accomplishment, they are foreigners in America and the values of America are foreign to them.

The insistence that black Americans stand outside the American experience contradicts the active part that they have played in the making of its institutions and the shaping of its culture. And looking forward rather than backward, our findings show that the overwhelming number of black Americans wish to be part of the larger American society, its imperfections notwithstanding, and are wholeheartedly committed to its central values. Their pride in their identity as blacks does not undercut, or limit, or qualify their overarching identity as Americans.

[175] We are here referring to some anonymous reviews of an earlier version of this manuscript.

T he Survey of Chicago African Americans was a telephone survey of African Americans 18 years of age or older residing in certain areas of the city of Chicago. The Survey Research Center at the University of California, Berkeley, conducted the survey in 1997 during the period from February 10 to August 3. Households were first screened for the presence of African American adult residents. If more than one resided there, a list was made of the eligible adults, and one was selected at random to be the respondent for the interview. The rate of successful screening was 78.7 percent. The rate of completion for interviews in eligible households was 71.8 percent. The product of those rates gives an overall response rate of 56.5 percent. There were 756 completed interviews.

Design of the Sample

Since it is very costly to screen a general population sample for members of a minority group, it was necessary to focus the study on areas known to have a high proportion of blacks. The sample was drawn in two different ways. One part was drawn from telephone directory listings in Chicago. The other part of the sample was a list-assisted random-digit sample of telephone numbers from those prefixes serving the area with a high proportion of blacks. Both parts of the sample were supplied by Genesys Systems.

DIRECTORY SAMPLE

Since it is very time consuming to call thousands of random telephone numbers and screen them for residential numbers and also for race, we hoped to increase the number of interviews that could be completed within the budget by using a directory sample for part of the overall sample. The directory portion of the sample was drawn from listings having a high probability of being located in a set of census tracts with 80 percent or more blacks, according to the 1990 Census.

The limitations of such a sample are well known, since only about half of all telephone numbers are listed in directories. Nevertheless, since we also have a random-digit telephone sample as part of the overall sample, it was possible to compare the results obtained from the two types of samples, to see if the directory sample was unacceptably biased. We did not find substantial differences between the two parts of the sample. In terms of respondent characteristics, we found that the main difference between the two samples was that the directory sample respondents were somewhat older than the random-digit respondents. The mean ages were, respectively, 51 and 44 years. Part of this difference, however, was due to the larger proportion of directory respondents living alone. After weighting to adjust for the differential number of eligible respondents in each household, the mean ages were, respectively, 48 and 43 years.

RANDOM-DIGIT SAMPLE

A random-digit sample is preferable to a directory sample since it will include households with telephone numbers that are not in the directory. Since, however, a simple random-digit telephone sample would contain mostly telephone numbers that are either out of service or are not residential, a list-assisted random-digit sample was drawn. In a list-assisted sample, the proportion of numbers that correspond to households is increased to 50 percent or more. For a detailed description of this sampling method, see Robert J. Casady and James M. Lepkowski, "Stratified Telephone Survey Designs," *Survey Methodology* 19 (June 1993), pp. 103–13. For this study, the stratum containing clusters of telephone numbers with no residential listings was omitted from the sample.

The list-assisted random-digit sample was drawn from those telephone prefixes having a high probability of being located in the same set of census tracts included in the directory portion of the overall sample—namely, those tracts with 80 percent or more blacks, again according to the 1990 Census.

Weights

Weights were created for each case to compensate for differences in probabilities of selection due to the variation in the number of eligible persons in a household and due to the use of two separate sampling frames.

WEIGHT TO ADJUST FOR NUMBER ELIGIBLE (*wt1*)

Since only one eligible black adult per household was selected to be interviewed, persons residing in households with more eligible persons were less likely to be selected than persons residing in households with fewer persons. The relative weight to compensate for this difference is P, where P is the number of eligible persons in the selected household (1–4 = *actual number*, and 5 = *5 or more*). This relative weight was then multiplied by a constant, to scale the weight so that the weighted number of cases equals the unweighted number of cases in the data file (756).

WEIGHT FOR LISTED AND FOR NUMBER ELIGIBLE (*wt2*)

Part of the sample was drawn from random telephone numbers, and another part was drawn from directory listings. The households with listed telephone numbers had a greater probability of being selected, since they could enter the sample from either of the two frames. The second weight is designed to compensate for that difference in the probability of selection.

When the random-digit sample was drawn, each selected telephone number was tagged to indicate whether or not it was also in the telephone directory. Based on that information, we estimated that approximately 70 percent of households in the survey area did not have listed telephone numbers. Accordingly, an adjustment factor was calculated for weighting down the number of cases sampled that had directory listings and for weighting up (relatively) the number of cases sampled that were not listed. The second weight for each case on the data file, *wt2*, is the product of this adjustment factor and the first weight, *wt1*. Note that this weight incorporates the adjustment (in *wt1*) for the number of eligible persons in the household. A constant was used to scale this second weight also, so that the number of weighted cases equals the unweighted number of cases in the data file (756). This second weight should generally be used for analysis of the data.

T his is a condensed version of the questionnaire used for computer-assisted telephone interviewing for the 1997 Survey of Chicago African Americans. Administrative and computer-oriented material is excluded, but all of the substantive material is contained here.

Many questions in this interview had two or more randomized versions. Depending on the value of a random number generated for each such question for each respondent, the computer-assisted interviewing system (CASES) would display the appropriate wording of the question to be read by the interviewer to the respondent. The values of the random numbers were stored in the data file and were then used to determine which version of a question each respondent answered.

Background Variables: Part 1

age
    Just to make sure we're talking to a representative cross section of
        people, we have a few questions for statistical purposes.
    How old were you on your last birthday?

gender
    INTERVIEWER CODE OR ASK AS NECESSARY: Are you male or female?

Feeling Thermometers

thm1
    These first questions are about some political leaders. I'll read a
        name and ask you to rate the person on a thermometer that runs

from zero (0) to one hundred (100). The higher the number, the warmer or more favorable you feel toward that person. The lower the number, the colder or less favorable you feel. If you feel neither warm nor cold toward them, rate that person a fifty.
How about Martin Luther King, Jr.? On a scale from zero to one hundred, how would you rate him?

thm2
How about
[VERSION 1] Louis Farrakhan?
[VERSION 2] Louis Farrakhan, the head of the Black Muslims?
On a scale from zero to one hundred, how would you rate him?

thm3
How about Jessie Jackson?
On a scale from zero to one hundred, how would you rate him?

Immigrants Experiment

imm1
Many different groups of people have come to the United States at different times in history. In recent years, the number of
[VERSION 1] Mexicans and other Hispanics
[VERSION 2] Koreans and other Asians
[VERSION 3] immigrants from countries in Africa has been increasing.

How likely do you think it is that the growing number of [GROUP] will cause taxes to increase because they will need more public services?

Would you say it is very likely, somewhat likely, not too likely, or not at all likely?

imm2
How likely do you think it is that
[VERSION 1] Mexicans and other Hispanics
[VERSION 2] Koreans and other Asians

[VERSION 3] immigrants from countries in Africa will take jobs away
from people who are already here?

Treatment of Various Groups

gr1a
These next questions are about what you think should be done
about some controversial issues.
(CHANGE RANDOMLY THE ETHNICITY: BLACK/JEWISH)

Suppose the [ETHNICITY] editor of a college newspaper was fired for
printing an article that criticized [OPPOSITE ETHNICITY] students on
campus.

How do you feel about firing the editor?
Are you in favor of, or opposed to, firing the editor?

(Follow-up in this series of questions:)
Are you strongly (in favor of/opposed to) this or only somewhat (in
favor/opposed)?

gr2a
How do you feel about allowing groups with extreme or radical
views to hold public rallies?

gr4a
In areas where a large number of
[VERSION 1] blacks
[VERSION 2] Mexican Americans live, how do you feel about chang-
ing the boundaries for congressional districts so that more
[GROUP] will be elected to Congress?

gr5a
How do you feel about boycotting businesses run by
[VERSION 1] Koreans
[VERSION 2] whites who are accused of taking advantage of black
customers?

gr6a

How do you feel about large companies having quotas to make
sure a certain number of
[VERSION 1] blacks
[VERSION 2] Mexican Americans are hired?

gr7a

How do you feel about giving free speech to groups that
express things that blacks and other minority groups find
insulting?

grt9

When you think about most whites who support affirmative action,
do you think their support shows that they really
have good will toward blacks, or does it simply show they're
supporting affirmative action because they feel they
have to?

College Entrance Experiment

gr10

Now I'm going to tell you about two young men who are applying
to college. George is black and his father is (CHANGE RANDOMLY:) a
doctor / out of work.

Sam is white and his father is (CHANGE RANDOMLY:) (also) a doctor /
(also) out of work.

On his college entrance exam, George scored (CHANGE
RANDOMLY:) 55/60/65/70/75 out of a possible 100
points.
Sam scored 80 out of a possible 100.

If the college can only accept one of the two young men, who do
you think should be admitted—George, because of the special
obstacles faced by blacks, or Sam, because his score on the
entrance exam was higher?

Trust and Reasons for Success: Forced Choices

tst1

These next questions are about people in general.

Do you think that, one, most people are willing to help others, or, two, that most people think only about themselves?

tst2

Do you think that, one, most people would take advantage of you if they had the chance, or, two, that most people would do their best to act decently?

tst3

Thinking about most people who
[VERSION 1] are rich
[VERSION 2] have developed their talents, do you think this is usually because, one, they have had more opportunities than most people, or, two, they made the most of what they had?

tst4

Thinking about most people who
[VERSION 1] are poor
[VERSION 2] haven't developed their talents, do you think this is usually because, one, they did not have the same opportunities as most people, or, two, they did not make the most of what they had?

Values: Importance of Each

v1

Now I'm going to ask you about a number of values. As I read each one, please tell me how important each one is as a guiding principle in your life.
How about achieving wealth, material possessions, and money?
Is that extremely important, very important, somewhat important, or not a very important guiding principle in your life?

v2

(How about) Faith in God?

v3

(How about) Freedom of speech?

v5

(How about) Self-discipline?

v7

(How about) Narrowing the gap between the rich and the poor?

v8

(How about) Protecting the environment?

v9

(How about) Increasing jobs and economic growth?

v10

(How about) Achieving economic security?

v12

(How about) Preserving tradition and respect for time-honored customs?

Social-Psychological Items

sps3

Now here are some statements about life in general. As I read each one, please tell me how much you agree or disagree.

How about, "The answers to this country's problems are much simpler than the experts would have us think?"

Do you agree strongly, agree somewhat, disagree somewhat, or disagree strongly with that statement?

sps4

How about, "It is important for friends to have similar opinions?"

sps5
> How about, "Most
> [VERSION 1]: whites
> [VERSION 2]: Jews don't have any respect for blacks?"

sps6
> (How about) "Obedience and respect for authority are the most
> important virtues children should learn?"

sps7
> (How about) "You sometimes can't help wondering whether any-
> thing is worthwhile anymore?"

sps8
> (How about) "If
> [VERSION 1] people
> [VERSION 2] Mexican Americans
> [VERSION 3] black Americans work hard enough, they can make a
> good life for themselves?"

sp10
> (How about) "A little practical experience is worth more than all
> the books put together?"

sp11
> (How about) "It makes sense to distrust those who act differently
> from most people?"

sp12
> (How about) "Nowadays a person has to live pretty much for
> today and let tomorrow take care of itself?"

sp13
> (How about) "The problem with groups like
> [VERSION 1] the Irish
> [VERSION 2] Jews is that now that they've made it in America, they
> want to pull up the ladder after them?"

sp14

>(How about) "To be successful, a group's members must act and think alike?"

sp16

>(How about) "Most
>[VERSION 1] whites
>[VERSION 2] Jews are basically racist?"

Values: Forced Choices

pg1a

>Now here are some values that everyone agrees are important. But sometimes we have to choose one value over another. If you absolutely had to choose between each of the following two values, which is more important?
>How about, one, working for the rights of women, or, two, preserving traditional family values?
>(If you had to choose between these two, which would you say is more important?)

pg1b

>Would you say that (VALUE CHOSEN) is much more important, somewhat more important, or only a little more important than (VALUE NOT CHOSEN)?
>(ALL VALUE QUESTIONS IN THIS SERIES HAVE THIS SAME FOLLOW-UP)

pg2a

>(How about) Guaranteeing law and order in society, or, guaranteeing individual freedom?

pg3a

>(How about) Being tough on criminals, or protecting the rights of those accused of crime?

pg4a

>(How about) Defending the community's standards of right and

wrong, or protecting the rights of individuals to live by their own
moral standards?

pg5a
(How about) Protecting the environment, or increasing jobs and
economic growth?

pg6a
(How about) Encouraging belief in God, or a modern scientific outlook?

pg7a
(How about) Being able to say what you think about public issues,
or being able to live in a safe society where the laws are
respected?

pg8a
(How about) Narrowing the gap between the rich and the poor, or
increasing economic growth?

Responsibility for Social Problems

cause
Some people say that racial discrimination is still the most
important cause of the problems that black Americans face
these days. Others say that the general breakdown of black
families is now the most important cause. What do you
think?
Are the problems blacks face these days still mostly caused by discrimination, or are they mostly caused by the breakdown of
many black families?

prb1
Now I'm going to read a list of problems facing black Americans
these days. As I read each one, please tell me who you think
should have the main responsibility for solving it.
How about increasing employment opportunities for black Americans?

Who should have the main responsibility for taking care of this, white Americans or black Americans?

prb3

How about solving the problem of drug use among black Americans in the inner cities?

Who should have the main responsibility for taking care of this, white Americans or black Americans?

Racial Conspiracy Items

csp1

Now here are some more statements. As I read each one please tell me if you agree strongly, agree somewhat, disagree somewhat, or disagree strongly.

How about, "The FBI and the CIA make sure that there is a steady supply of guns and drugs in the inner city?"

csp2

(How about)

[VERSION 1] "Louis Farrakhan, the head of the Black Muslims, is basically

[VERSION 2] "Historically, it is

correct that Jews were a major factor in financing and organizing the slave trade in the 17th and 18th centuries?"

csp3

(How about) "White doctors created the AIDS virus in a laboratory and released it into black neighborhoods?"

csp4

(How about)

[VERSION 1] "It

[VERSION 2] "Louis Farrakhan, the head of the Black Muslims,

may be a little extreme to describe Jews as 'blood suckers', but there's a lot of truth to it all the same?"

Racial Values: Forced Choices

rcv1
> In thinking about the needs of black Americans today, do you think the civil rights movement should focus, one, mostly on the problems of poor blacks, or, two, should it focus equally on the problems of middle-class *and* poor blacks?

rcv2
> In general, do you think it's better for people of different races, one, to keep to themselves as much as possible, or, two, to live and work together so they can learn to understand each other?

rcv3
> To make real progress in achieving equality, is it better for blacks, one, to work together with whites, or, two, to work together mostly with other blacks?

rcv4
> As things now stand, is it more important to, one, treat blacks and whites the same, or, two, to first overcome the effects of past discrimination?

rcv5
> Is it more important, one, to promote racial harmony between blacks and whites, or, two, for blacks to fight for their rights, even if it means creating tension between blacks and whites?

rcv6
> Is it more important, one, to support freedom of expression, or, two, to stop people from saying negative things about blacks?

rcv7
> Is it more important, one, to help those who are worse-off, regardless of their color, or, two, to concentrate on helping blacks?

rcv8

Is it more important, one, to promote black culture as a separate culture, or, two, to emphasize what Americans have in common?

rcv9

Is it more important, one, for blacks to build good relations with whites, or, two, for blacks to build pride and respect for themselves, even if it means causing tension between blacks and whites?

rc10

Is it more important, one, for schools in black neighborhoods to hire black teachers, or, two, for these schools to select the most competent teachers regardless of race?

Black Identification and Nationalism

rcid

How much do you think what happens to blacks in this country will affect your life: a lot, some, a little, or not at all?

bn1

Now, as I read each of the following statements, please tell me how much you agree or disagree.
How about, "Blacks should always vote for black candidates when they run for an elected office?"
Do you agree strongly, agree somewhat, disagree somewhat, or disagree strongly with that statement?

bn2

(How about) "Blacks are better off living with other blacks in black neighborhoods rather than living with whites?"

bn3

(How about) "Black people should shop in stores owned by other blacks whenever possible?"

bn4

(How about) "Blacks should have control over the economy in
mostly black communities?"

bn5

(How about) "African wise men who lived hundreds of years ago
do not get enough credit for their contributions to modern
science?"

bn6

(How about) "The ancient Greek philosophers copied many ideas
from black philosophers who lived in Egypt?"

Psychological Tolerance and Self-Esteem

pt1

As I read each of the following statements, please tell me whether
you think it's basically true or basically false.
How about, "Most people are honest chiefly through fear of getting caught?"
Do you think that is basically true, or basically false?

pt2

(How about) "Most people inwardly dislike putting themselves out
to help other people?"

pt3

(How about) "With things going as they are, it's pretty hard to
keep up hope of amounting to anything?"

pt4

(How about) "Most people make friends because friends are likely
to be useful to them?"

pt5

(How about) "I often feel that I have been punished without
cause?"

pt6
> (How about) "When in a group of people, I usually do what the others want rather than make suggestions?"

pt7
> (How about) "I would have been more successful if people had given me a fair chance?"

pt8
> (How about) "I certainly feel useless at times?"

pt9
> (How about) "It bothers me that so many
> [VERSION 1] Korean
> [VERSION 2] black store owners take advantage of black customers?"

pt10
> (How about) "Teachers often expect too much work from their students?"

pt11
> (How about) "I commonly wonder what hidden reason another person may have for doing something nice for me?"

pt12
> (How about) "Jews have too much power
> [VERSION 1] in business and banking?"
> [VERSION 2] in the entertainment industry?"
> [VERSION 3] in the government?"

pt13
> (How about) "It bothers me to see new immigrants from
> [VERSION 1] Europe
> [VERSION 2] Mexico
> [VERSION 3] Asia getting more breaks than black Americans who were born here?"

Anti-Semitism

jw1
> Speaking generally about Jews, please tell me how much you agree
> or disagree with the following statements.
> How about, "Most Jews are ambitious and work hard to succeed?"
> Do you agree strongly, agree somewhat, disagree somewhat, or
> disagree strongly?

jw2
> (How about) "Most Jews are more willing than other people to use
> shady practices to get ahead in life?"

jw3
> (How about) "Most Jews believe that they are better than other
> people?"

jw4
> (How about) "Most Jews are inclined to be more loyal to Israel than
> to America?"

jw5
> (How about) "Most Jews don't care what happens to people who
> aren't Jewish?"

Attitudes Toward Homosexuals

hm1a
> How do you feel about laws that are designed to protect homosexuals
> from job discrimination? Are you in favor of, or opposed to, this?
> (Follow-up:) Are you strongly (in favor of/opposed to) this, or only
> somewhat (in favor/opposed)?

hm2a
> How do you feel about homosexuals and lesbians being allowed to
> adopt children? Are you in favor of, or opposed to, this?

hm3a

How much do you agree or disagree with the statement, "Homosexuality is disgusting"? Do you agree strongly, agree somewhat, disagree somewhat, or disagree strongly?

Political Identification

pid

Generally speaking, do you usually think of yourself as a Democrat, a Republican, an Independent, or what?

(If Democrat or Republican:) Would you call yourself a strong Democrat/Republican, or a not very strong Democrat/Republican?

(If neither:) Do you think of yourself as closer to the Democratic Party or closer to the Republican Party?

ideo

Generally speaking, would you consider yourself to be a liberal, a conservative, a moderate, or haven't you thought much about this?

(If liberal or conservative:) Do you think of yourself as a strong liberal/conservative, or a not very strong liberal/conservative?

(If neither:) Do you think of yourself as more like a liberal or more like a conservative?

Political Knowledge

inf1

Now for some questions about the federal government. Which party has the most members in the House of Representatives in Washington?

inf2

How much of a majority is required for the U.S. Senate and House of Representatives to override a presidential veto:
one-half plus one vote, three-fifths, two-thirds, or
three-quarters?

inf3
> In general, thinking about the political parties in Washington, would you say Democrats are more conservative than Republicans, or Republicans are more conservative than Democrats?

inf4
> Whose responsibility is it to determine if a law is constitutional or not: is it the President, Congress, or the Supreme Court?

Religious Practice

relig
> What is your present religious preference? Is it Protestant, Catholic, Islam, Jehovah's Witness, or something else?
> INTERVIEWER: CODE OR ASK IF NECESSARY
> What church or denomination is that?

gide
> Would you say religion provides some guidance in your day-to-day living, quite a bit of guidance, or a great deal of guidance in your day-to-day life?

fchurch
> How often have you attended religious services of any kind in the last 12 months: at least once a week, two or three times a month, about once a month, a few times, once, or never?

fpray
> IF NEVER ATTENDED RELIGIOUS SERVICES IN LAST 12 MONTHS: How often do you pray or read the Bible? ALL OTHERS: Not counting the time when you're attending religious services, how often do you pray or read the Bible: at least once a day, a few times a week, once a week, a few times a month, or less often than that?

Childhood Family Structure

biop
> These next questions are about your family. At the time you were
> born, was your mother married to your biological father?
> (If not:) Was your mother ever married to your biological father?

livw
> Who did you live with most of the time while you were growing
> up: with both of your biological or natural parents, with only one
> biological or natural parent, or with someone else?
> (If only one:) Was that your mother or your father? (If someone
> else, skip to 'fema')

spo1
> Was your (mother/father) married during most of the time while you
> were growing up or wasn't (she/he) married for most of that time?
> (If not:) Was (she/he) living with someone in a marriage-like rela-
> tionship (but not legally married) during most of the time you
> were growing up?

fema
> CODE OR ASK AS NECESSARY: Who did you live with most of the time
> you were growing up?

wynm
> ASKED IF RESPONDENT LIVED WITH ONLY BIO FATHER AND HE WAS EVER MARRIED
> TO BIO MOTHER; OTHERS SKIP TO 'WYND'.
> Why didn't you live with your biological mother (most of the time)
> when you were growing up? Did your mother and father sepa-
> rate because of divorce, did she die, or was it because of some
> other reason?

wynd
> ASKED IF RESPONDENT LIVED WITH ONLY BIO MOTHER AND SHE WAS EVER MARRIED
> TO BIO FATHER; OTHERS SKIP TO 'WHRM'.
> Why didn't you live with your biological father (most of the time)

when you were growing up? Did your mother and father separate because of divorce, did he die, or was it because of some other reason?

whrm

ASKED IF RESPONDENT DID NOT LIVE WITH BIO MOM MOST OF THE TIME AND BIO MOM NOT DECEASED; OTHERS SKIP TO 'WHRD'.

Where was your biological mother during most of time you were growing up: in the same city where you lived, not in the same city, but in the same state, or someplace else?

whrd

ASKED IF RESPONDENT DID NOT LIVE WITH BIO DAD MOST OF THE TIME AND BIO DAD NOT DECEASED; OTHERS SKIP TO 'MARITAL'.

Where was your biological father during most of time you were growing up: in the same city where you lived, not in the same city, but in the same state, or someplace else?

Background Variables: Part 2

marital

Are you currently married, living with someone in a marriage-like relationship but not legally married, separated, divorced, widowed, or have you never been married?

(If living with someone:) Have you ever been married?

(If married or ever married:) How many times have you been married (including your present marriage)?

mnd1

IF RESPONDENT HAS BEEN PREVIOUSLY MARRIED:

How did your (last) marriage end? Were you divorced or widowed?

state

In what state were you born?

educ

What is the highest grade or year of school you completed?

empl
> Are you currently employed full-time, employed part-time, unemployed, retired, a student, keeping house, or what?

isum
> What is your annual family income?
> Think of the income *before* taxes of all members of your household living with you now. Include income from all sources, including wages, dividends, interest, pensions, and other sources.

fin1
> When it comes to your financial situation these days, would you say you are better-off now than you were a year ago, worse-off now, or are things about the same as they were a year ago?

fin5
> Looking ahead five years from now, do you think your financial situation will be better than it is now, worse, or about the same as it is now?
> (END OF INTERVIEW: Thanks for your cooperation)

Bibliography

Adorno, Theodor, Else Frenkel-Brunswick, Daniel Levinson, and R. Nevitt Sanford. 1950. *The Authoritarian Personality*. New York: Harper.

Allen, Richard L. 2001. *The Concept of Self: A Study of Black Identity and Self-Esteem*. Detroit, Mich.: Wayne State University Press.

Allen, Richard L., Michael C. Dawson, and Ronald E. Brown. 1989. A Schema-Based Approach to Modeling an African-American Racial Belief System. *American Political Science Review* 83:421–41.

Anderson, Barbara A., Brian D. Silver, and Paul R. Abramson. 1988a. The Effects of Race of the Interviewer on Measures of Electoral Participation by Blacks in SRC National Election Studies. *Public Opinion Quarterly* 52:53–83.

———. 1988b. The Effects of the Race of the Interviewer on Black-Related Attitudes of Black Respondents in SRC/CPS National Election Studies. *Public Opinion Quarterly* 52:289–324.

Banks, William M. 1996. *Black Intellectuals: Race and Responsibility in American Life*. New York: Norton.

Barry, Brian M. 1965. *Political Argument*. New York: Humanities Press.

Berlin, Isaiah. 1969. Two Concepts of Liberty. In *Four Essays on Liberty*. New York: Oxford University Press.

Berman, Paul, ed. 1994. *Blacks and Jews: Alliances and Arguments*. New York: Delta.

Bernal, Martin. 1987. *Black Athena: The Afroasiatic Roots of Classical Civilization*. New Brunswick, N.J.: Rutgers University Press.

———. 2001. *Black Athena Writes Back: Martin Bernal Responds to His Critics*, ed. David Chioni Moore. Durham: Duke University Press.

Bledsoe, Timothy, Susan Welch, Lee Sigelman, and Michael Combs. 1995. Residential Context and Racial Solidarity among African-Americans. *American Journal of Political Science* 39:434–58.

Bobo, Lawrence, and Vincent L. Hutchings. 1996. Perceptions of Racial Group Competition: Extending Blumer's Theory of Group Position to a Multiracial Social Context. *American Sociological Review* 61: 951–72.

Bowen, William G., and Derek Bok. 1998. *The Shape of the River: Long-Term*

Consequences of Considering Race in College and University Admissions. Princeton, N.J.: Princeton University Press.

Brewer, Marilynn B. 2001. Ingroup Identification and Intergroup Conflict: When Does Ingroup Love Become Outgroup Hate? In R. Ashmore, L. Jussim, and D. Wilder, eds., *Social Identity, Intergroup Conflict, and Conflict Reduction.* New York: Oxford University Press.

Cannato, Vincent J. 2001. *The Ungovernable City: John Lindsey and His Struggle to Save New York.* New York: Basic Books.

Converse, Philip E. 1964. The Nature of Belief Systems in Mass Publics. In David E. Apter, ed., *Ideology and Discontent.* New York: Free Press.

Cose, Ellis. 1993. *The Rage of a Privileged Class.* New York: HarperCollins.

Cronon, Edmund D. 1969. *Black Moses: The Story of Marcus Garvey and the Universal Negro Improvement Association.* Madison, Wis.: University of Wisconsin Press.

Davis, Darren W. 1997a. The Direction of Race-of-Interviewer Effects among African-Americans: Donning the Black Mask. *American Journal of Political Science* 41:309–22.

———. 1997b. Nonrandom Measurement Error and Race of Interviewer Effects among African Americans. *Public Opinion Quarterly* 61: 183–207.

Dawson, Michael C. 1994. *Behind The Mule: Race and Class in African-American Politics.* Princeton, N.J.: Princeton University Press.

———. 2001. *Black Visions: The Roots of Contemporary African-American Political Ideologies.* Chicago: University of Chicago Press.

Dinnerstein, Leonard. 1994. *Anti-Semitism in America.* New York: Oxford University Press.

Duckitt, John. 1992. *The Social Psychology of Prejudice.* New York: Praeger.

Evanzz, Karl. 1999. *The Messenger: The Rise and Fall of Elijah Muhammad.* New York: Vintage Books.

Fine, Gary Alan, and Patricia A. Turner. 2001. *Whispers on the Color Line: Rumor and Race in America.* Berkeley: University of California Press.

Finkel, Steven E., Thomas M. Guterbock, and Marian J. Borg. 1991. Race-of-Interviewer Effects in a Preelection Poll: Virginia 1989. *Public Opinion Quarterly* 55:313–30.

Franklin, V. P., Nancy L. Grant, Harold M. Kletnick, and Genna Rae McNeil, eds. 1998. *African Americans and Jews in the Twentieth Century: Studies in Convergence and Conflict.* Columbia, Mo.: University of Missouri Press.

Gerard, Harold B. 1988. School Desegregation: The Social Science Role. In Phyllis A. Katz and Dalmas A. Taylor, eds. *Eliminating Racism: Profiles in Controversy.* New York: Plenum Press.

Glazer, Nathan. 1997. *We Are All Multiculturalists Now.* Cambridge, Mass.: Harvard University Press.

Glock, Charles Y., and Rodney Stark. 1966. *Christian Beliefs and Anti-Semitism.* New York: Harper & Row.

Gurin, Patricia. 1985. Women's Gender Consciousness. *Public Opinion Quarterly* 49:143–63.

Gurin, Patricia, Shirley J. Hatchett, and James S. Jackson. 1989. *Hope and Independence: Blacks' Responses to Electoral Party Politics*. New York: Russell Sage Foundation.

Hardin, Russell. 1995. *One for All: The Logic of Group Conflict*. Princeton, N.J.: Princeton University Press.

Hatchett, Shirley, and Howard Schuman. 1975–76. White Respondents and Race-of-Interviewer Effects. *Public Opinion Quarterly* 39:523–28.

Herring, Mary, Thomas B. Jankowsi, and Ronald E. Brown. 1999. Pro-black Doesn't Mean Anti-white: The Structure of African-American Group Identity. *The Journal of Politics* 61:363–86.

Hochschild, Jennifer L. 1995. *Facing Up To The American Dream: Race, Class, and the Soul of the Nation*. Princeton, N.J.: Princeton University Press.

Hofstadter, Richard. 1967. *The Paranoid Style in American Politics*. New York: Vintage Books.

Howe, Stephen. 1998. *Afrocentrism: Mythical Pasts and Imagined Homes*. New York: Verso.

Jaynes, Gerald David, and Robin M. Williams, Jr., eds. 1989. *A Common Destiny: Blacks and American Society*. Washington, D.C.: National Academy Press.

Kaufman, Jonathan. 1988. *Broken Alliance: The Turbulent Times between Blacks and Jews in America*. New York: Charles Scribner's Sons.

Kinder, Donald R., and Nicholas Winter. 2001. Exploring the Racial Divide: Blacks, Whites, and Opinion on National Policy. *American Journal of Political Science* 45:439–57.

Kiss, Elizabeth. 1996. Five Theses on Nationalism. In Ian Shapiro and Russell Hardin, eds., *Political Order*. New York: New York University Press.

Kuklinski, James, Michael D. Cobb, and Martin Gilens. 1997. Racial Attitudes and the "New South." *The Journal of Politics* 59:323–49.

Lee, Jennifer. 2002. *Civility in the City: Blacks, Jews, and Koreans in Urban America*. Cambridge, Mass.: Harvard University Press.

Lefkowitz, Mary. 1996. *Not Out of Africa: How Afrocentrism Became an Excuse to Teach Myth as History*. New York: Basic Books.

Lefkowitz, Mary R., and Guy MacLean Rogers, eds. 1996. *Black Athena Revisited*. Chapel Hill: University of North Carolina Press.

Lerner, Michael, and Cornel West. 1995. *Jews and Blacks: Let the Healing Begin*. New York: G. P. Putnam's Sons.

Lewis, David Levering. 1993. *W. E. B. Du Bois: Biography of a Race, 1868–1919*. New York: Henry Holt and Company.

———. 2000. *W. E. B. Du Bois: The Fight for Equality and the American Century, 1919–1963*. New York: Henry Holt and Company.

Malcomson, Scott L. 2000. *One Drop of Blood: The American Misadventure of Race*. New York: Farrar, Strauss and Giroux.

Markus, Hazel Rose, Claude M. Steele, and Dorothy M. Steele. 2000. Color-Blindness as a Barrier to Inclusion: Assimilation and Nonimmigrant Minorities. *Daedalus* 4:233–57.

Martire, Gregory, and Ruth Clark. 1982. *Anti-Semitism in the 1980s*. New York: Praeger.

Marx, Gary. 1967. *Protest and Prejudice*. New York: Harper & Row.

McClosky, Herbert, and Alida Brill. 1983. *Dimensions of Tolerance: What Americans Believe about Civil Liberties*. New York: Russell Sage Foundation.

McClosky, Herbert, Paul J. Hoffmann, and Rosemary O'Hara. 1960. Issue Conflict and Consensus among Party Leaders and Followers. *American Political Science Review* 54:406–27.

McClosky, Herbert, and John H. Schaar. 1965. Psychological Dimensions of Anomy. *American Sociological Review* 30:14–40.

McFadden, Robert D., Ralph Blumenthal, M. A. Farber, E. R. Shipp, Charles Strum, and Craig Wolff. 1990. *Outrage: The Story behind the Tawana Brawley Hoax*. New York: Bantam.

McWhorter, John, H. 2000. *Losing the Race: Self-Sabotage in Black America*. New York: Free Press.

Miller, Arthur H., Patricia Gurin, Gerald Gurin, Okasana Malanchuk. 1981. Group Consciousness and Political Participation. *American Journal of Political Science* 25:494–511.

Myrdal, Gunnar. 1944. *An American Dilemma*. New York: Harper & Brothers.

Oliver, Melvin L., and Thomas M. Shapiro. 1995. *Black Wealth/White Wealth: A New Perspective on Racial Inequality*. New York: Routledge.

Patterson, James T. 2001. *Brown v. Board of Education: A Civil Rights Milestone and Its Troubled Legacy*. New York: Oxford University Press.

Patterson, Orlando. 1997. *The Ordeal of Integration: Progress and Resentment in America's "Racial" Crisis*. Washington, D.C.: Counterpoint/Civitas.

Pearson, Hugh. 1994. *The Shadow of the Panther: Huey Newton and the Price of Black Power in America*. Reading, Mass.: Addison-Wesley.

Quinley, Harold E., and Charles Y. Glock. 1977. *Anti-Semitism in America*. New York: Free Press.

Ravitch, Diane. 1974. *The Great School Wars*. New York: Basic Books.

Reed, Adolph, Jr. 1999. *Stirrings in the Jug: Black Politics in the Post-Segregation Era*. Minneapolis: University of Minnesota Press.

Rhea, Joseph Tilden. 1997. *Race Pride and the American Identity*. Cambridge, Mass.: Harvard University Press.

Rieder, Jonathan. 1985. *Canarsie: The Jews and Italians of Brooklyn against Liberalism*. Cambridge, Mass.: Harvard University Press.

Rosenberg, Morris, and Roberta G. Simmons. 1971. *Black and White Self-Esteem: The Urban School Child*. Washington, D.C.: American Sociological Association.

Schaeffer, Nora Cate. 1980. Evaluating Race-of-Interviewer Effects in a National Survey. *Sociological Methods and Research* 8:400–419.

Schuman, Howard, and Jean M. Converse. 1971. Effects of Black and White Interviewers on Black Responses in 1968. *Public Opinion Quarterly* 35:44–68.

Schuman, Howard, and Stanley Presser. 1981. *Questions and Answers in Attitude Surveys: Experiments on Question Form, Wording, and Context.* New York: Academic Press, Inc.

Scott, Daryl Michael. 1997. *Contempt and Pity: Social Policy and the Image of the Damaged Black Psyche 1880–1996.* Chapel Hill: University of North Carolina Press.

Selznick, Gertrude, and Stephen Steinberg. 1969. *The Tenacity of Prejudice: Anti-Semitism in Contemporary America.* New York: Harper & Row.

Sigelman, Lee, and Susan Welch. 1991. *Black Americans' Views of Racial Inequality: The Dream Deferred.* New York: Cambridge University Press.

Sigelman, Lee, James Shockey, and Carol K. Sigelman. 1993. Ethnic Stereotyping: A Black-White Comparison. In Paul M. Sniderman, Philip E. Tetlock, and Edward G. Carmines, eds., *Prejudice, Politics and the American Dilemma.* Stanford: Stanford University Press.

Sniderman, Paul M., Richard A. Brody, and Philip E. Tetlock, eds. 1991. *Reasoning and Choice: Explorations in Political Psychology.* New York: Cambridge University Press.

Sniderman, Paul M., and Edward G. Carmines. 1997. *Reaching Beyond Race.* Cambridge, Mass.: Harvard University Press.

Sniderman, Paul M., Pierangelo Peri, Rui J. P. de Figueiredo, Jr., and Thomas Piazza. 2000. *The Outsider: Prejudice and Politics in Italy.* Princeton, N.J.: Princeton University Press.

Sniderman, Paul M., and Thomas Piazza. 1993. *The Scar of Race.* Cambridge, Mass.: Harvard University Press.

Stouffer, Samuel Andrew. 1992. *Communism, Conformity, and Civil Liberties: A Cross-Section of the Nation Speaks Its Mind.* 2d ed. New Brunswick, N.J.: Transactions Publishers.

Sullivan, John L., James Piereson, and George E. Marcus. 1982. *Political Tolerance and American Democracy.* Chicago: University of Chicago Press.

Swain, Carol M., Robert R. Rodgers, and Bernard W. Silverman. 2000. Life after Bakke Where Whites and Blacks Agree: Public Support for Fairness in Educational Opportunities. *Harvard BlackLetter Law Journal* 16:147–84.

Tate, Katherine. 1991. Black Political Participation in the 1984 and 1988 Presidential Elections. *American Political Science Review* 85:1159–76.

———. 1993. *From Protest to Politics: The New Black Voters in American Politics.* Cambridge, Mass.: Harvard University Press.

Taylor, Charles. 1994. *Multiculturalism: Examining the Politics of Recognition,* edited and introduced by Amy Gutmann. Princeton, N.J.: Princeton University Press.

Triandis, Harry C. 1988. The Future of Pluralism Revisited. In Phyllis A. Katz and Dalmas A. Taylor, eds., *Eliminating Racism: Profiles in Controversy*. New York: Plenum Press.

Triandis, Harry C., ed. 1976. *Variations in Black and White Perceptions of the Social Environment*. Urbana: University of Illinois Press.

Tucker, Clyde. 1983. Interviewer Effects in Telephone Surveys. *Public Opinion Quarterly* 47:84–95.

Turner, Patricia A. 1993. *I Heard It through the Grapevine: Rumor in African-American Culture*. Berkeley: University of California Press.

Walker, Clarence Earl. 2001. *We Can't Go Home Again: An Argument about Afrocentrism*. New York: Oxford University Press.

Welch, Susan, Lee Sigelman, Timothy Bledsoe, and Michael Combs. 2001. *Race & Place: Race Relations in an American City*. New York: Cambridge University Press.

West, Cornel. 1993. *Race Matters*. Boston: Beacon Press.

Zaller, John. 1992. *The Nature and Origins of Mass Opinion*. New York: Cambridge University Press.